MURDER BY NUMBERS

Perspectives on Serial Sexual Violence

Lawrence J. Simon, M.S.

ATHENA PRESS
LONDON

MURDER BY NUMBERS:
Perspectives on Serial Sexual Violence
Copyright © Lawrence J. Simon, M.S. 2002

All Rights Reserved

ISBN 1 932077-46-4

First Published 2002 by
MINERVA PUBLISHING CO.
1001 Brickell Bay Drive, Suite 2310
Miami, Florida 33131

Published 2003 by
ATHENA PRESS
Queen's House, 2 Holly Road
Twickenham TW1 4EG
United Kingdom

Printed for Athena Press

MURDER BY NUMBERS
Perspectives on Serial Sexual Violence

Inspired by Monica L.M.

ACKNOWLEDGEMENTS

I've been writing this book since 1997. Many people have contributed to its thought content throughout my years of experience within the social science field. First and foremost was my mentor, Dr. James Tabeling, who has paved the way toward writing this book and has provided me with a sound foundation in psychoanalytical thought as it applies to the realms of violent behavior. Some of his ideas and shared knowledge directed me as a catalyst during the early writings of the book.

Special thanks: Dr. Tom Rosenbaum, who has provided me with knowledge and confidence in speaking with and building respect with incarcerated inmates. Elisa Corrado, who has provided me with a broad perspective of humanity as it applies to violence and criminal behavior. Carlos Martinez, who has given me an opportunity to share my thoughts and show a respect for my own theoretical perspectives.

I was inspired to expand some of the writings of this book and apply it to realms of serial violence by attending various lectures. First and foremost was Gregg McCrary's lecture on the violent mind. His knowledge and experience as a former FBI supervisory agent has provided me with a vision into some of the young violent men's thought processes I've encountered during my past experiences.

I would like to thank the entire social worker staff and administrators at the Dade County Public Defenders Office. Dr. William Bickard for giving me an opportunity to work with his staff. Dr. Barton Jones, a friend who has provided me with valuable information within the field of forensic psychology. I would like to thank the young men who were incarcerated in various prisons throughout the United States.

The production of this book would be null and void without their assistance into some of the causes of their behavior. Throughout the entire book I've made an important and necessary effort to keep their names confidential to ensure their privacy.

Most of all, I would like to show my deepest gratitude to my mother, Melanie Simon, who has provided me with support and confidence to publish my work. She has been there with me through all its trials and tribulations. I would like to extend my deepest love to my entire family for their support throughout my life. You cannot gauge the importance of having a family that shows a greater love for any son, grandson, cousin, or brother. To speak merely of gratitude is not enough to show my thanks and appreciation for the work they endured.

ABOUT THE AUTHOR

Lawrence J. Simon briefly formed a behavioral-assessment consulting firm for law enforcement agencies throughout the United States and Canada known as LJS International, before he was employed as an investigative specialist for the Broward County Sheriff's Office in Ft. Lauderdale, Florida. There Mr. Simon is in charge of investigating allegations of physical and sexual abuse of victims of eighteen years and younger throughout Broward County. Mr. Simon has a Bachelor's degree in psychology at Eastern Michigan University, a Master's degree in science at Nova Southeastern University, and a Master's degree in psychology at the Miami Institute of Psychology, where he's finishing his doctoral degree in both forensic psychology and neuropsychological studies. He has worked at the Milan Federal Correctional Institution just outside Detroit, Michigan. While enrolled in the forensic program, Lawrence J. Simon has worked with the Date County Public Defenders Office Juvenile Sentencing Project, associated and funded by the US Department of Justice, where he conducted research and behavioral investigative analysis on juvenile sexual offenders in the felony adult criminal justice system. Mr. Simon has attended and received accreditation in numerous seminars, namely "The Violent Mind", "Assessing and Managing Violence Risk", and "Assessing Risk in Sex Offenders", to name a few.

ABOUT THE BOOK

This book focuses on sadistic fantasy and sexual violence from a cognitive and psychoanalytical perspective. Hence, it presents both past and present theoretical data regarding the conscious and unconscious motivation of documented serial rapists and killers. One of the books related to *Murder by Numbers* is *Journey into Darkness* by John Douglas and Mark Olshanker. This particular book takes the reader into the mind of a serial killer through the eyes of FBI agent John Douglas. It discusses actual cases that the FBI has handled and the stories of the killers and their victims. The sequel to *Journey into Darkness* is a book titled *Mind Hunter*. *Mind Hunter* follows a similar plot as *Journey into Darkness*. In the former book, authors John Douglas and Mark Olshanker take the reader deep inside the FBI's elite serial crime unit. It is a disturbing look at this country's most brutal murderers. On reading this book, one cannot comprehend the evil of men who walk among us.

Some of the contents delivered in *Murder by Numbers* are based on the two previous books mentioned. This book touches on some of the new bravados in crime, including but not limited to juvenile violence, stalking and serial sexual murder. Also, *Murder by Numbers* is one of the first comprehensive books to offer an in-depth analysis on serial crime and violence from a psychoanalytical perspective. Hence, the book includes rare footage and documentation from cases that haven't been read about in books or seen on television.

This is not the manifested Hollywood version of violence. It's the real thing that author Lawrence J. Simon introduces to his readers. Now, in mystifying detail, the legendary serial killer's sexual manifestations are explored before, during and after the chilling encounters he has with his victims and the mess he always leaves behind. The author takes the reader into the dark places he's been and uncovers some of the hidden mysteries behind violent crime, beyond the steel gates of prison, inside the psychiatric wards of jails and within the social spectrum of both the men and women who've committed some of the most unthinkable acts of violence. Explore the domain of violence from the mouths of the perpetrators, who act on its behalf.

Contents

PREFACE

We are not a people who harvest the notion of what is right and wrong. We tune to the internal light that makes us human, yet binds our eyes to the eternal depths of darkness for we hold the truth of our sexual being and the evil that manifests itself in the ambience of pain.

Holding true to mankind's essence is the entity created in his image… VIOLENCE. I wake up every morning dreading the day I leave for work. I expect to see something new and absorb the pain of both the perpetrator and the victim: a human atrocity, a murder, a car jacking, a rape, and such like. Sometimes you're unable to place a name, a face, or a punishment to crime. Violence just happens and I submerge myself every day into the pathologies that linger in the mindset of those who commit it. This book offers a graphic look into the unconscious motivations of violence told by some of the most violent men encountered both in and out of prison.

What goes through a serial killer or serial rapist's mind as he watches his victims lie helpless before he stabs, mutilates, rapes, beats, or strangles them to death? Does he wish to see them suffer? Does he want to see the fear in their eyes before they die? Or does he wish to be loved at that very instant? The answers to these questions and more reveal themselves in each of the chapters.

I cannot put a name or a face to the inspiration of this book. However, one incident has stuck in my mind as I began writing my book almost two years ago. The following story is just one incident to a landmark of violence sweeping across all corners of the world.

December 1997, the ice and snow put a permanent glaze over my car. I didn't want to leave for the correctional facility that day. I had a bad feeling before I arrived through the steel doors that separated what I call freedom from hell. Early that morning an inmate was referred to the psychology department by one of the correctional officers working the late shift the previous morning. He was a thirty-six-year-old heavy-set man serving a life sentence for the brutal murder of his wife of fifteen years. I worked with this man for almost three months and I listened to his painful recollections of how his life really was.

One of the first things he said to me was, "I killed the bitch because she always made me feel like shit." I couldn't help but empathize with the pain and humiliation he was subjected to on a daily basis. He left for work and the thoughts of his wife's verbal abuse attacked his entire mindset. He quotes, "It was like a steel compressor always bearing down on my chest." This man had no previous history of violence or criminal activity. Other people described his disposition as passive and in control of his emotions. However, for almost thirteen years he went to work wishing he never came home. Nobody ever identified with this man's pain.

Reportedly, his wife told him he'd never amount to anything and that he could never make her happy. A month before he murdered his wife he recalled an incident when he was about to have sex with his wife and was unable to maintain an erection. She impatiently left the bedroom in disgust and said to him, "I'd rather sleep on the couch than sleep with the most worthless man I've ever known." He remembered those words and said, "It got much worse after that." He said she came home from work late every night and made fun of him because he couldn't get an erection. He quotes, "Man, she never lived that night down."

One Thursday, early morning at approximately 3:30 A.M. he walked into the living room where his wife lay sleeping on the couch and strangled her to death with a wire hanger. He remembered the look in his wife's eyes as she gasped her last breath of air. He quotes, "She had a look of shock, like she couldn't believe I would do it." He was finally relieved when he killed his wife and he hasn't had any regrets ever since. He told me I was the first person he'd ever told this story to. Could you imagine what it was like for this man to have nobody to talk to? When the door shut at the end of our last session I didn't realize it was the last time I would ever see him again. About two weeks later he swallowed the sharp end of a screwdriver and bled to death internally. The next morning correctional staff found him motionless in the corner of his cell.

The next question I ask is, what separates mankind from being a ruthless cold-blooded killer? Like the inmate previously discussed, is it years of being subjected to verbal and emotional abuse? Or does the answer reveal itself through the estranged personality of an inept human being? Does the answer lie in man's absolute threshold for anger? In other words, how much can one tolerate before hurting someone?

There's a difference between wishing someone dead and actually committing the crime of murder. Can you ever recall being very upset at a person on the highway? So angry that you wanted them to disappear? Would you envision that person's car blowing up on the highway? Did you envision the person in the car blowing up? Did you see the person's arms and legs thrown across the highway?

Before answering these questions we must understand the differences between thought processes of normal behavior that perhaps divides us from psychosis, being potentially psychotic and existing as a neutral force.

A man who exists farthest from reality is more likely to possess psychotic thought patterns. For example, think of a person cutting you off on the road and nearly killing you and your family. A natural response to the incident is a feeling of anger. Whether or not you respond aggressively depends on if the incident caused you to exceed your tolerance levels. A primary defense mechanism against acting aggressively is the guilt you may possess afterwards.

Again, directly fixating your anger on a stranger who cuts you off the road is a natural response to an aversive situation. However, being obsessed daily with the thoughts of that person blowing up signifies a psychotic or perhaps delusional state of mind. If you follow the driver home and methodically plan his death and act on it, you exist in the realm of psychosis. And the term "psychosis" is just an illusion. It's an illusion we are unable to experience unless we've seen it in the light of our own eyes. For example, the moon appears closer than it really is. A psychotic may see it as a moving object that appears directly in front of his/her face.

Psychotic impulses and violent thought processes exist as separate entities but can coexist together. If we possess psychotic impulses then psychotic thought processes are likely to occupy the same space. However, violent thought processes don't have to occupy psychotic impulses. In a serial killer's case, psychotic impulses are likely to precipitate sadistic fantasy or vice versa. Putting that aside, let's look at a situation where psychotic thought processes and impulses also conflict with one another but coexist together. Think of a man who brutally rapes and murders your thirteen-year-old daughter. This is a tricky situation because you face difficult circumstances related to your daughter's murder. However, if you methodically plan to kill the man who raped your daughter (psychotic impulse), then together you must possess the psychotic thought processes necessary to carry out the act itself. There must be a certain degree of psychotic thought processes and impulses to methodically plan a murder, regardless of the situation, such as revenge for your daughter.

Once an individual possesses psychotic impulses, there's a fifty-fifty chance he or she will act aggressively on its behalf. The degree of control has a lot to do with the person's defense mechanisms, level of guilt for hurting someone and the situation that precipitates the anger.

The entity of a serial killer's impulse stems much further than the conflict between good and evil. The thoughts he has on killing someone exists in a repertoire of impulses that connects itself to fantasy and the internal belief of what he's becoming.

Only half of his actions are explained in the eyes of conscious thought. His impulses and thought processes change minute to minute, hour to hour, and day to day. They change from low, medium and high frequency aggressive impulses. These impulses are regulated by situations that surround his unique environment existing as past and present circumstances. Hence, negative stimuli from the environment cause his impulses or thought patterns to fluctuate, which inevitably create mood swings and increase his insatiable appetite to hurt others.

This can happen to any one of us. The higher our aggressive impulses the more they preoccupy our lives and the further it distances us from our ideal mode, which often keeps us at bay.

High aggressive impulses are regulated by our normal state of being. If they weren't, then we wouldn't be able to function because our bodies would be under constant physiological stress. The anxiety created by high aggressive impulses causes improper judgment in most situations. For example, can you be so angry at a person that it causes you to do things you regret? Think about it. Have you ever had aggressive impulses that have been so intense that it caused you to strike a person without thinking? The difference between striking that person, letting it go and killing that person depends on how you filter your aggressive impulse during that specific time. The longer you keep the impulse inside, the more violent is the behavior when you finally release it. Some people keep the aggressive impulses inside for so long they depersonalize themselves from others. Hence, the human target becomes easier to strike.

Lost in a Wilderness

Throughout this chapter I want my readers to picture my friend's story as their own in the hope of understanding the developmental process of a would-be serial killer.

I was nine years old when Tony was my best friend. We both grew up in Detroit, Michigan. I remember he used to tell me strange things about his parents. He told me how his mother and father used to take turns coming into his bedroom at night to tuck him in. He told me his father used to take his pants down and play with his penis before falling asleep. In the morning, before school, his mother would perform fellatio on his penis. After school, his father came home drunk and beat him with a ping-pong paddle. Later, after his father beat him he would tell Tony to take his pants off and everything would be okay. Tony's father told him to perform fellatio on him. If he didn't then his father would beat him again.

It's hard to imagine a story and a situation such as this. I still wonder what would have happened if I told someone the day I heard Tony's unsuspecting cry for help. A few months later Tony told the same stories to his fifth grade teacher and he was taken away from his parents by Human Resource Services (HRS).

I hadn't seen or heard from Tony in about twenty years until last week when he called me from a maximum-security prison. We talked for a few minutes. He mentioned how he had killed two pretty girls at a local college where he and I used to go. He told me how he ripped off their clothes and forced them to give him fellatio. He held them hostage for hours with a knife and at gunpoint before killing them. He strangled both female victims. When they were deceased he cut them into pieces and kept their body parts.

I couldn't believe this was a close friend of mine. He lived a block from my house and we used to hang out together in elementary school. Twenty years later I heard from him in prison only to find he's a convicted killer currently serving two life sentences for multiple homicide.

When I hung up the phone and the initial shock wore off I looked back and remembered the way he was treated by his parents. I remember thinking, if the abuse he suffered was so intense that he could've never recovered fully from it.

I started to talk with Tony while he was at the prison and in the process I've learned more about what was and what is going on in his mind. I guess I was sparked by my own curiosity about a friend of mine who seemed normal at one time.

He told me about how he used to stalk his victims. He would follow them for days and even weeks before attacking them. There were other times he wasn't so strategic. Sometimes he thought about killing people on the spur of the moment. If Tony saw the opportunity he took it. For example, if he saw a young girl walking alone in an uncrowded area, he watched and waited a little until the parent slipped off and left the girl alone or unguarded.

After hearing Tony's gripping stories of murder I began formulating my own hypothesis about why he killed and what went on in his mind during his ruthless killing spree. What I found was most interesting, because you can attribute my findings to most serial killers.

Tony, as with most would-be or "actual" serial killers, filtered his aggressive impulses by killing people who were associated with the pain he had once felt either consciously or unconsciously during the past or present. The pain is so intense their thought processes linger around the issues of guilt, anger and manic-depression. Episodes of mania precipitate an attack on another and depression occurs before or after the attack. Guilt formulates as an unconscious process to be alive but they feel no remorse for their victims.

As the killer stalks his victim, he's reliving the fantasy of killing the person before it actually happens by envisioning his initial approach. Envisioning the approach stimulates him sexually, drawing him closer to the victim. When a killer strikes he must possess a certain degree of high aggressive impulses. Without these impulses, he is unable to kill another human being because killing is an aggressive act. As the killer strikes his first blow there are mixed feelings of anger, frustration and resentment that predominate his psyche.

What drives the killer to kill again is the sexual gratification achieved through looking at the victim's facial expression at the time he or she is being attacked. An overblown sense of power, accomplishment, control and dissatisfaction together create an insatiable urge to kill again.

Each victim that the killer selects fulfills some sort of an unfulfilled childhood sexual fantasy that creeps its way into adulthood. I say childhood because the killer isn't functioning as an adult and his thought processes linger at the stage he's fixated at.

For example, one day Tony pre-selected a little boy as his victim. The boy was nearly the same age as Tony when he was abused by his parents. Tony projected his own anger and guilt onto the boy before he attempted to end his life. Instead of just having sex with the boy as he did with all his other victims, he talked to him rather pervertedly. He told the boy to touch his penis. When he wouldn't do it then Tony touched the boy's penis. Tony asked the boy if he enjoyed touching his penis. Regardless of the boy's answer Tony almost beat him to death.

Later, Tony told me he felt bad after beating the boy. He was the only victim Tony felt bad for attacking. He felt guilty because he said the boy reminded him of himself during the time he was abused. The boy had no connection with Tony's life as a child. In fact, the boy had both loving and caring parents before he was sexually assaulted by Tony. What happened in this case is that Tony created his own script about the boy's life in relation to his own. Most killers create their own story about their victims' lives and this usually has some relation with their own lives or in connection with their fantasy.

Later, Tony told me that he made it as quick and as painless as possible when he finally killed the little boy. He shot him in the head and buried him in the woods. He never told anyone about this before, apart from me. Why did Tony feel bad for killing the boy? Well, Tony saw himself through the boy's eyes. During the time of the murder, Tony felt like he was doing the boy a favor by killing him. This is how Tony must have felt during the time of his abuse. After the abuse, Tony felt sorry for himself. The guilt he felt was so intense the only way he functioned was by killing others in the hope of gaining satisfaction and purpose to his life.

Tony used the boy to reenact the same sequence of events from the past in order to recreate a desired outcome to his present story. First, Tony touched the boy's penis and then asked the boy to touch his. Once the sexual encounter was initiated and completed it was too late for the boy. Tony felt he had to kill him because this is what Tony wanted to do to himself when he was that age. Here is a poem Tony wrote before he murdered his second female victim.

> I crave to see the witness of death,
> for the eyes can reveal the sounds of her last breath.
> I need to feel the lost love of her pounding heart
> The flesh that surrounds her lips have torn us apart.
> Now I must cradle the blood that surrounds the water
> never regretful for the death of his daughter.

Tony began killing pretty young coeds in the range of fourteen to twenty-five years of age. He said that killing girls gave him some sort of power and temporary control over his life. Tony has never been able to manage the guilty feelings about the events that occurred in his past.

Tony relieved his emotional pain and guilt from his past by stalking young girls and killing them in violent ways. The victims Tony chooses unconsciously represent his mother, father and himself. Whoever the victim Tony chooses is the person he associated with pain in his past life and present circumstances.

He was extremely violent towards the women he killed. The coroner stated in his autopsy report that the two young women were raped and stabbed repeatedly. This indicated to me that Tony's anger might have been associated with women.

21

What stuck out in my mind almost immediately was the abuse Tony suffered at the hands of his mother. He used his female victims for revenge against his mother for what she did or failed to do with him when he was a child.

Tony's repressed angry feelings began to foster intense anxiety. Over time, this anxiety became so intense that it led to aggressive impulses. These hostile impulses assumed total control over his ego functioning. Therefore, Tony's ego surrendered all judgment to his emotions. At this point, Tony's psyche was governed entirely by his emotions. Since his steady emotional state was anger, then this was the emotion that would surface in reality. Tony's psychotic impulses were caused by the steady build up of guilt, resentment and anger about unresolved issues of the past that led up to difficulties in coping with the present.

Next, Tony disassociated himself from society. He became a time bomb waiting to explode. Some people handle themselves differently during times of intense stress. Tony coped with high levels of stress and anxiety by killing people. He was able to keep himself together by making sense out of the people he killed. The people he killed served their purpose as a masturbating tool for success, power, control and momentary satisfaction.

Killing Methods

Tony was very particular in the methods he used to kill his victims. Remember, every victim he chose was a means to fulfill a sexual fantasy. The methods he used to kill his victims fulfilled that same sexual fantasy and it was constantly relived while masturbating. Tony's victims would be tied up for hours or even days at a time. He raped and beat them until he got bored.

The less time he strategically planned out his kill the quicker he ended the victim's life.

Death was either caused by strangulation and/or stabbing. Every one of Tony's female victims was cut up after death. He stalked them, pushed them into his car, gagged them, and drove out to a secluded area and raped them. After that he continued to rape them until he was tired. When he was finished with the victim he killed them with a cutting tool or by strangulation. When they were dead he continued to have sex with their corpses.

After killing his victims he cut the flesh off their upper thigh. He performed this ritual in order to fulfill a sexual fantasy. His sexual fantasies had something to do with the dismemberment of body parts. When he masturbated he envisioned his female victims struggling until they lost an arm or leg.

While Tony masturbated in his room he relived the killings of his victims until he reached an orgasm.

Tony selected pretty women for a number of reasons. First, it has already been established he had angry feelings towards his mother for what she did to him in the past. She should have never allowed the abuse to happen, let alone be the primary cause of it. Tony felt he couldn't have pretty women because of his mother's emotional abuse. He chose pretty women to relive a dream he thought could never happen.

Secondly, women make an easy target. Men are able to gain control over women rather quickly because of their physical strength. Even though Tony did manage to kill a few young men, he did so because they were in the way of his primary target.

Why were there no rituals performed on the men whom Tony killed? Saying it was easier and quicker for Tony to use a gun would be an easy answer to a difficult question. In Tony's case, he infrequently killed men for reasons other than their being in the way.

One of the reasons was that it was difficult for Tony to accept his father as a sexual deviant. It was much easier for Tony to accept his mother as sexually deviant because during the time of his abuse he unconsciously wished to have sexual relations with his mother. To this day, Tony represses his guilty feelings for having these wishes. His guilty feelings were eventually transformed into rage during the time when Tony's mother attempted to have sexual relations with him. As an adult, Tony projects the anger created by his mother onto his innocent victims.

He reenacts his unconscious wish and motivations in order to be the aggressor instead of the victim. He transforms himself into the aggressor by initiating sexual contact with his female victims. Tony's sexual activity towards his victims after death (post-mortem) reflects hidden homosexual impulses.

When Tony's victims were dead it was safe for him to display his own erotic nature. His father used to beat Tony before having sexual relations with him. Here is an example of Tony's unconscious processes of hidden homosexual desire. When father is dead he can no longer have sexual relations with me; I will beat him senseless until he is dead so I can have sexual relations with him. Tony uses the corpses to display his unconscious wish to have sex with his father.

Tony cut tiny pieces of flesh from specific areas of his female victims in order to masturbate later. During masturbation, he would imagine a specific body part being attacked by an animal. The animal in the fantasy would be Tony himself. Once again, Tony was the predator, the victim would be the prey.

What motivated Tony to kill again and again is not only the sexual gratification and sense of control it gave him then but also the relief it gave him from his past and who he was becoming in the present?

When Tony would kill his high aggressive impulse shifted from a guilty state of mind into aggression. Tony then became preoccupied with his thoughts and emotions. As a result, revenge became a subliminal message of an unconscious motivation in Tony's thought process. The only way to keep himself from falling into a deep depressive state was to keep killing.

Not only did killing give him relief from anxiety, but it

provided him with a sexual outlet. The only other alternative he was left with was killing himself.

Deep inside, most serial killers are miserable and often depressed. Instead of possessing normal symptoms of depression they often become psychotic.

Many serial killers are antisocial and manic-depressive individuals. They find relief in killing people who are connected to the pain they're feeling.

In the beginning, Tony's motivation to kill was to seek revenge from his past. Later, it shifted from sexual relief to emotional gratification during the present. Most serial killers have a strong sense of accomplishment regarding their work. He becomes proud of what he does. A formidable aura of "cockiness" overcomes his personality. Not only is he cocky for not being caught but he believes he's invulnerable.

Most serial killers, as in Tony's case, are recipients of abuse themselves. Some will kill their victims in a similar manner in which they were abused. The killer can either be consciously or unconsciously aware of this phenomenon. For example, a person who rapes his victims before killing them was very likely a recipient of physical or sexual abuse. These individuals can be emotionally confused as well as possessing a psychiatric illness.

Part of Tony's psyche accepted the sexual abuse from both his parents because it signified his own wish fulfillment. As a result he felt guilty for accepting the abuse as part of a wish that inevitably came true.

When a killer like Tony attacks, he projects his own feelings onto his victim by believing her wish is to be sexually molested. As a result, the killer expresses his disagreement and anger towards the victim for believing she wishes to be abused.

Why does the killer believe the victim wishes to be sexually abused? What is the killer so angry about?

Let's answer these questions keeping Tony's case in mind. Tony is guilty for wishing to be sexually molested by his mother when he was a child. The wish is unacceptable to his ego and it is repressed. He creates his own anger and frustration when he attacks his victim because he is not able to deal with his internal conflicts. He unconsciously acts out on his aggressive impulses by having sexual relations with his victim. Tony's psychotic thought processes lead him to believe his victim enjoys the sexual abuse. Therefore, because Tony believes his victim enjoys the sexual abuse he or she must die and take his place.

When Tony struck his victim he essentially struck himself. Hence, the victim would become connected with Tony's thought processes. Tony believed he was doing his victim a favor by killing her because that was what he wished for during the time he was abused.

Another part of the killer's unconscious mind shows resentment for his parents' actions. The killer's feelings of resentment towards his parents can be filtered through many different facets in his life. If guilt is one of the facets being filtered then the person will probably not kill anyone. What will happen is that they will likely go on to establish unstable relationships. Either partner in the relationship is likely to be a recipient of extreme emotional and/or physical abuse. It all starts from the abused person projecting his or her guilty feelings onto the partner in the relationship.

If unconscious guilt and resentment shift into feelings of intense anger (high energy impulses) then the person becomes vulnerable to his emotions. What happens is that the person surrenders his judgment of reality and exists in his own fantasy world governed by his emotions. When this happens, physical abuse occurs in and/or outside a relationship. If a person becomes completely preoccupied with his/her anger and hostile emotions, he/she becomes unpredictable and often ends up being violent. Depending on the state of mind he or she is in, in relation to the intensity of anger he/she feels can sometimes throw him/her into a desperation act. Hence, we now enter the mind of a mass murderer.

Mass murderers will go on a rampage and kill anything in

sight at that moment. It's difficult to catch them alive because they usually end their own lives in the process of their rampage.

Mass murderers are completely controlled by their emotions and often become completely disconnected with reality. The only reality they see is through the eyes of their angry emotions.

To look inside the minds of serial killers and mass murderers, it is vital to first look into the personality structure of a normal functioning human being.

Personality Structure

The organization of a personality is arranged in an apparatus of three structures, called the dream mode, reality mode and the previously mentioned ideal mode. These structures are separate and distinct from each other but can coexist within one psyche at a given time or space. Each one of the structures develops at birth and follows through the course of the entire life.

The black hole of the unconscious releases energy (mental impulses), which fluctuates between the dream, reality and ideal modes. The mode that contains the most energy directed by the black hole of the unconscious determines the actions of an individual's behavior (see diagram on opposite page).

The definition of the dream mode is the positive or negative mental representation of an event or fantasy before it actually occurs. For example, you're in a nightclub and you see a beautiful young woman staring at you. You want to go up and talk to her but there are many self-defeating thoughts running through your mind. For instance, you say to yourself, "I'll look like a fool, she won't like me. I'll get beaten up by her boyfriend. I'm too ugly for her." There are many other thoughts that can keep you away from talking to this beautiful girl. Each thought has its purpose and represents some important aspects of your life.

You can also have positive interpretations of what will

happen if you talk to this girl. For instance, what if she finds me attractive? What if she wants me to talk to her? What if she wants to go out on a date with me? Still, even with these positive interpretations you currently exist within the dream mode because you have not yet talked with her. There are some people who remain comfortably in the dream mode. These people are afraid of reality or what they perceive reality to be. These people can be the recipients of physical and/or emotional abuse. Rather than face reality, they run from it because running is what protected them during the time of the abuse. Think about it. If you are sexually abused by a parent or sibling you try to make sense out of what's happening. To do so, you create your own reality by permanently placing yourself in a dream mode. You learn to do whatever it takes to avoid reality because you don't want to face what happened to you as a child. Hence, defense mechanisms are employed.

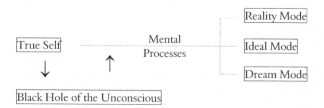

- Mental Processes are shaped by our perceptions of the environment, our experiences and ourselves.

- The Black Hole of the Unconscious is the energy from which our mental processes are born and which fluctuates as a result of experiences within the environment and a constant striving to stay ahead.

- True Self is a human being who remains untouched or un-influenced by the world that surrounds him or her.

- Mental processes approaching the Reality Mode produce behavior that is consistent with what really is and what society considers normal and abnormal.

- Mental processes approaching the Dream Mode produce behavior that is consistent with fantasy and the art of becoming.

- Mental processes approaching the Ideal Mode produce behavior that is consistent with how you perceive yourself and the world as it relates to your true state of being and personality. For example, if you always had a passion for working with animals and you find yourself down the road working with oil tankers you're functioning outside your Ideal Mode and in this case within the Reality Mode. The more materialistic possessions we have the further we distance ourselves from our Ideal Mode.

Violence can occur when a person's ideal mode is breached by either situational experience, environmental factors such as social inadequacies and/or our own perceptions of powerlessness and low self-worth. Hence, the mental processes released from the black hole of the unconscious are harnessed in a particular mode in the form of shame, guilt and envy. This energy remains dormant at one particular mode or fluctuates between the three modes sending messages that negatively affect the view of one's self. Hence, many times these views are projected onto the victim.

Sexual violence in the reality mode is formulated by the pressures of conformity. Such individuals exclusively exist on an external basis in the reality mode but do so against their will. These individuals are not afraid to confront reality by internalizing it but are afraid to unmask it to the public. Hence, underground sexual sadists inflict intense pain on their victims but secretly. They are somewhat concerned for their partner's welfare. However, they accept the reality of their sexual desires and engage in violent behavior that brings about sexual pleasures.

Sexual violence in the dream mode is formulated by envy. These individuals are deliberate in their acts of violence and are fueled by their inner fantasies and a sense of powerlessness in the world. They wish to become something else by taking something valuable from another. Rapists who exist in the dream mode are almost always fueled by the wish to feel powerful and desired by the victim. Anger is usually produced once the dream mode is breached.

Sexual violence in the ideal mode is formulated as a result of feeling inferior and projecting those feelings onto other people in the environment in a sexual manner. Many of the rapists who exist in the ideal mode inflict intense physical and emotional pain on their victims. The rapist is already angry for who he perceives himself to be. Hence, his feelings of inadequacy are almost always projected onto his victim. He doesn't envy his victim. He blames her for not accepting him for who he perceives himself to be. This individual is in conflict with what he perceives himself to be and where he is in life. Ted Bundy is one example who fits in this mode. His anger toward women was believed to begin after his girlfriend in college abruptly ended a romantic relationship with him, thus breaking his heart. Later, experts came to realize that some of Bundy's victims partially resembled his ex-girlfriend's physical features.

The reality mode is your negative and/or positive thought processes of an event or fantasy only after it occurs. For example, say you go ahead and start talking to the beautiful girl staring at you in the nightclub. You say, "Hi," introduce yourself, offer her a drink. She says, "No, thank you." About ten seconds later she walks away. A positive interpretation of what happened during that moment would be for you to say, "She likes me, she's playing hard to get." A negative interpretation would be, "She finds me unattractive, she thinks I'm a loser, and my breath smells bad."

To see how sexual violence is applied to each mode, please review the preceding diagram. The difference between the dream mode and reality mode is that you have the reality of the situation to deal with. You've already talked to the pretty girl in the nightclub. Now, it's up to you to act consistently with the reality of what transpired in the conversation. People who exist in the reality mode are willing to take chances with their lives. For instance, take a person who gambles. Before he puts down his bet he thinks about whether or not the time is right (dream mode). If it is the right time he will put a substantial amount of money on the table. Win or lose, the positive and negative interpretations of the event that transpired place this person in the reality mode because the situation has already taken place.

The ideal mode is an event or fantasy that is somehow associated with your true identity. Your actions in this mode are direct representations of your true self: for example, being a leader and not a follower. Your true identity is developed around you and the family during your childhood years. If you once loved being around animals then you should still want to be around animals. People who exist in the ideal mode enjoy careers that are consistent with their true character and personality. For example, if you've gone through psychoanalysis when you were younger it wouldn't be surprising if you took up the field in the future. If you loved animals as a kid it wouldn't be surprising if you were to become a veterinarian or a park ranger. The reality and fantasies of your true feelings, thoughts, and emotions need to coexist together within your psyche in order to exist in the ideal mode.

Function of Personality

Our personalities function according to the state of mind we currently exist in. Our states of mind can abruptly shift direction by the fluctuating patterns within the brain that creates conflict between the three modes. For example, one minute we feel good about something and the next minute we feel lousy.

The fluctuating patterns are unpredictable because they are a result of the many situations we encounter during our lifetime. They can shift from minute to minute, hour to hour, day to day, week to week, month to month and year to year. As a result of unpredictable situations created within our environment, the fluctuating patterns produce erratic behaviors that are not always consistent with our true identity (ideal mode). It's not healthy to be separated from our ideal mode. Any separation can cause brief lapses of anxiety and neurotic behaviors. The longer we remain separated from our ideal mode the worse it gets.

The major difference between a mode and a state of mind is that our state of mind shifts much quicker than a mode does.

The state of mind is what drives us to feel a certain way at any given moment. The mode is what drives us to react and behave towards a situation at any given moment. For example, why did you step on an ant one day, and on another day save an ant from drowning? When you killed the ant the first time you had had a bad experience at work and you got into a big fight with your girlfriend. At the moment just before you step on the ant, you are in a hostile state of mind concurrent within the dream mode. After you take out your aggression and kill the ant, you now are in a relaxing state of mind concurrent with the reality mode.

Finally, when a behavior is consistent with your true identity you exist in the ideal mode. For example, consciously or unconsciously the ant represents something pure and it's not in your nature to kill something pure. However, if you do kill the ant, then your hostile state of mind gains complete control over your true self. A positive or negative state of mind that is not consistent with your true identity can distance you from maintaining control of your actions that are relevant to your ideal mode.

The final outcome of any behavior is predicated on the mode that harnesses the most amount of energy released from the black hole of the unconscious. The example I used in the previous paragraph rests upon the decision to kill the ant or to let it live. Regardless of your decision the energy exists within the dream mode because you haven't committed to the reality of letting the ant live or die. When you finally make your decision to kill the ant or walk away, most of the energy released by the black hole of the unconscious now exists in the reality mode. This is when you make your own interpretations about the reality of a situation. A normal person recognizes the reality of the ant lying dead next to you or saving its life by walking away. If perhaps on another day, for whatever reason, you save an ant from drowning in a pool, if this behavior is consistent with your true identity then most of your energy lies within the ideal mode. This is good because your actions and behavior are consistent with your true self. As a result, there is no room to feel guilty about your decisions.

Note, it is extremely difficult to exist within the ideal mode as we enter adulthood because we have to "go against the grain", so to speak, between the reality mode, dream mode and states of mind in which we exist, in order to find the hidden mental processes that comprise our total sense of being. The more possessions we own and responsibilities we have, it further distances us from our true identity. During childhood and adolescence we didn't own our possessions and have major responsibilities, so it was easier to behave consistently with our true selves. When we enter adulthood we are confronted with important responsibilities that are necessary for our survival. We have to worry about money, food, clothes and a roof over our heads. Along with the worries and responsibilities of caring for others and ourselves come the possessions such as owning a car, a house, clothes, and so on. When we reach this point we're not interested in connecting with our ideal mode. Instead, we are more interested in keeping our possessions, doing whatever it takes to survive, and leading a comfortable lifestyle. A good way to get in touch with our ideal mode is to go on a long fishing trip, or go camping in the Canadian wilderness for at least a month. We need to get away and no longer listen to the world that has distanced us from ourselves. Only the voices of nature can carry us away from the distractions of dreaming reality and living reality. Come on, didn't you ever just want to hop on the back of a Harley and head off into the sunset with nothing on you except a backpack?

Human Development

A human being develops from the mental processes inherited at birth by the black hole of the unconscious. These mental processes branch off into separate directions forming the dream, reality and ideal modes. From infancy to old age we possess certain character-logical traits of each mode.

Depending on our age, weight of responsibility and number of possessions, it becomes relevant to the mode we remain fixated in. The black hole of the unconscious, which is essentially the ideal mode, produces a predetermined amount of energy that is equally dispersed throughout the reality, dream, and ideal modes. When presented with different situations throughout our lives these fixed units of energy exist unevenly across the boundaries of the dream, reality and ideal modes. As a result, sporadic behavior frequently develops out of context with our true self. Depending on the mode that currently harnesses the most amount of energy will determine our behavior. For example, if most of the energy from the black hole of the unconscious lies within our reality mode, then we are proactive in encountering situations. We're the person who puts that bet down on the table. Regardless of the outcome of the bet, the person is maintained in the reality mode because the bet took place.

If most of our energy is in the dream mode, we more often than not fear reality. As a defense we attempt to create our own reality by manipulating the reality of the environment that surrounds us. This is done by imagining the outcome of scenarios we encounter. For example, we think to ourselves, *if I hand in an important document a day late I will be penalized*; or, *if I quit my job today then I will eventually starve*; or, you can say, *if I quit my job today I'll find a better one.* The truth is, we're not conscious of the outcome of our own reality because it doesn't exist yet. People who can't accept the fact they don't always know what's going to happen will create their own scenarios to events that occur: for example, writing a bibliography about the events of our life before they happen.

For each person to lead a successful and normal life there has to be an appropriate balance of energy distributed across the three different modes, particularly the ideal mode. You don't want to have all your energy exist in the ideal mode. Otherwise you surrender reality. Your lifestyle tends to fall into a morbid state.

Most serial killers' energy lies within the dream and reality modes. In a sense their reality is created by their dream mode. This is one of the reasons why serial killers are so difficult to catch. What happened to Tony and most serial killers is that almost all their energy released from the black hole of the unconscious lay dormant within the dream mode. The mental impulses lay in the dream mode for an extended period of time because their past and present lives were too intense to bring into the reality mode.

In Tony's case, his ideal mode was stripped away from him by his parents. As a child, Tony was completely traumatized by them. Remember, infancy, childhood and adolescence are the time when you're supposed to capture the essence of your true self. If denied access to your ideal mode the end result could lead to confusion in the future. As a result, you may find yourself behaving sporadically from one situation to the next. You find yourself fluctuating between both good and evil states of mind. The end result of all this can lead to depression, anxiety and the development of neurotic behavior.

The onset of abnormal development occurs when an act or interpretation of behavior is not true to our identity: for example, being in a career that represses a side of your true personality, like becoming an engineer when your passion is writing romance novels.

Up to the age of twenty-five our fantasies and behavior are consistent with who we are. Between the age of twenty-five and forty our choices are usually not consistent with our true identity. Note that the ideal, dream and reality modes are capable of producing their own abnormal behavior.

Abnormal behavior can develop at any time during the dream mode as a result of becoming preoccupied with mental representations, events and fantasies and never acting on them as a result of fear. I refer to this phenomenon as the reality deficit. For instance, before you ask your boss for a raise you create your own mental interpretations of what will transpire. If your interpretations are negative you might "chicken out" and never ask the boss for that raise.

If you do ask the boss for a raise regardless of your mental interpretations before the event you exist in the reality mode. Your boss replies, "You are doing a fine job so come to see me next week." Once in the reality mode you make your own mental interpretations of what just took place. A logical or healthy interpretation of what your boss said would indicate you have at least a fifty per cent chance of getting that raise. An illogical or unhealthy interpretation of the event would be thinking your boss is going to fire you next week. I call this phenomenon the "reality conflict" which is conducive to its off-balance and paranoid thinking. The reality conflict may also partially explain a serial killer's tendency to feel little or no remorse for his victims. Its thought content can go as far as to the serial killer believing he is already dead.

Abnormal behavior and fantasies develop within the three modes if at any time our thought processes are not consistent with our true identity or ideal mode. To get in touch with our ideal mode one can meditate, work out or, say, visit the wilderness. The following is an example of an abnormal thought process conducive to the ideal mode.

It's rush-hour traffic, you've had a terrible day at work, you're hungry and you can't wait to get home. Out of nowhere a stranger cuts you off and almost causes you to get into a five-car accident.

A natural feeling of anger is almost immediate after the incident. The anger should begin to dissipate a few minutes after the incident. Of course, it depends on the state of mind or mood you're in. When the anger does eventually dissipate after a few minutes your behavior is relative to the ideal mode. However, if you don't forget about the incident and it carries into the next day an idealized psychosis takes shape. This occurs when anger from a particular event projects itself onto other events transforming your thought patterns into chaotic and delusional fantasies. In this case, the anger from the highway incident carried over into the next day and you have fantasies about killing the person who cut you off. If these fantasies are acted out by following the person home, planting a bomb underneath his or her car, and watching them blow up, you have entered into a phase of psychotic behavior.

If there is a complete separation from the ideal mode it will put you in an idealized psychotic state of mind and it causes you to commit violent acts towards yourself and perhaps another individual.

How can we change? People can change by becoming aware of their own behavior as a result of the mode they exist in. The idea is to behave and indulge in activities consistent with their true identity. This can be difficult to achieve because society can restrict a person. For example, if we have the sudden urge to run away to the wilderness for two months, in most cases our job will not allow it.

What if we don't know what our true identity is? We search our hearts and minds and remember what we enjoyed as a kid. Remember, when we are young we follow the behavioral patterns of our ideal mode. As we get older we tend to lose them. When we become aware and are in control of our behavior in each mode we feel comfortable and satisfied within ourselves regarding the decisions we make every day in order to keep in touch with our true self.

January, 1998

INTRODUCTION

He said he used to bite the heads off frogs. This is what an inmate on D–block told me while serving two life sentences for the rape and murder of a six-year-old boy. The inmate spoke in tears that his father used to hold him down while he and his friend had sex with him from behind. He remembered how he wanted to die and that he tried to kill himself by swallowing a half-gallon of bleach. He was locked in his bedroom for days without food and water. If he wasn't in bed by the time his father came home he was beaten up so badly, he had difficulty chewing food for days. He remembered when he was eleven years old that his father came home drunk and stabbed him in the forehead. Instead of taking him to the emergency room, his father raped the boy repeatedly in his bedroom. "I will never forget what happened. I remember all that blood on my sheets."

I'm not going to harvest a restricted version of what I deal with on a daily basis. If I do that I'm cheating you out of the harsh realities of humanity as I see it. The stories I listen to regarding physical and emotional abuse are indeed heartbreaking. I empathize with intense amounts of pain and anguish for the abused and his victim caught in the crossfire.

I've experienced ambiences of pain during my life, yet I found myself shielded by the foundation of love and respect from society, to the degree of forming intimate relationships with parents, teachers, friends and significant others. In the midst of my sudden incursion into the forensic arena, I was delivered into the hands of intolerable hate, anger and frustration.

On a daily basis I absorb the pain of individuals who have either been abused or neglected at the discretion of society.

This is including but not limited to a parent or parents, teachers and significant others who have either lost touch with themselves, or have not been able to establish effective recourse with their own children. Hence, the foundation of love, trust and respect – that was perhaps lost in their life – now applies to their children and so on.

Some of the commonalities of adolescents I speak to are that their primary care givers deny them the natural right to a healthy existence, either by extreme neglect, emotional and physical abuse, to name but some. Instead of parents and significant others providing stepping stones for positive growth, nurturance and self-worth, some of these parents unconsciously harbor and project negative aspects of themselves and their lives onto their children.

One of the most important phases of attachment during childhood is the relationship established with parents, or in most cases that I come across, a single parent. The relationship I speak of is one of the forerunners into the internal dynamics of our maturing personalities.

Some experts believe that if you don't get along with your parents it's extremely difficult to establish long-lasting and meaningful relationships with an intimate partner. This isn't true in every case, but in most cases it is so. Ask yourself as to how many people exist in past and pre-existing relationships that have either failed, faltered, or lack a certain degree of worth?

For the most part, we model our parents' behavior while growing up under the umbrella of their past and present existence. Their verbal and non-verbal behavior patterns become familiarly absorbed, and later on are stored in our long-term memory banks. Hence, we never forget the way we were treated and almost certainly find ourselves many years down the road behaving identically as our parents did with us. As a result, we sometimes project our learned ideals and behavior patterns onto our children and our children's children.

How does this happen and what does this mean for the intensive purposes of the book? This happens as a result of being a "programmed species". Most people believe that we are unique, in the sense we are born and are each an individual person, possessing separate ideologies than others, and we therefore think and behave differently from anyone else. My belief is that we're born into a system created by our parents, peers, role models, culture and our interpretation of the role we have in society. Hence, our unique personalities form as a result of our interpretation of the system and where we fit within it. From the day we learn to walk, talk, form concrete operations and learn deductive reasoning skills our lives exist as an entity that binds us to family, society, culture, and peers. Our existence is predicated on a general acceptance of this system and vice versa. This includes forming unique personalities and self-esteem through reading the Bible, rules and morals created in the image of our parents, formations of role models, God, and our outlook on society. Indirectly, someone passed their thinking on to ours via our parents, grandparents, the media and so on.

In certain situations humanity and its behavior are not universal. Hence, in many cases they're unique and completely different from anyone born in this world. This is how the uniqueness of an individual's personality is classified and established within the context of humanistic psychology. Humanists believe that the formation of our personalities is an endless process that's created each day we experience life.

Holding true to their beliefs, look at the notorious categories of serial killers and mass murderers. The two are somewhat different regarding their general classification. However, the individuality and subjective thought processes of each make them even more distant, relative to the context in which they exist and experience life. We must remember that no serial killer or mass murderer, hence the term, is ever born into this role. They have somehow reached a point where the final circulation of air is cut off, leaving them destitute for life and in the shadow of their own madness.

A universal theme that places us, or at the very least, invites us into the path of violence is referred to as anger. Anger is one of the prerequisites leading to violent behavior, just as HIV leads to AIDS. Anger is an ingredient for violence. However, violence is not the end result of anger and anger doesn't necessarily always lead to violence. So what separates us from violent criminals? Experience leads me to believe it's the way we "tolerate" or "displace" anger, thus allowing our protective factors to reject the thought of violent action against others. These protective factors can include objects, people, places and cognitive processes. Most of the violent inmates I've interviewed lack these protective factors.

Quite simply, most of us either alter, project, or repress anger in a variety of ways that may exclude us from initiating violence on human targets. In many instances, anger in which we perhaps know and understand the dynamics is projected in a variety of ways other than in the form of physical violence. For example, some of us may have had sex with a partner of no significance other than to meet the immediate need of sexual gratification.

Sometimes the aggression created during sex is manifested in certain dimensions of anger, but in this case the anger is facilitated through the act of having sex and the human target doesn't necessarily, in a legal sense, become a victim of violence.

The cause for concern both ethically and legally is when the sexual act is dominated by intense surges of anger and hostility. Hence, the end result of the act leads to, and perhaps causes, severe physical and emotional injury.

Within a similar context of the previous discussion, people who commit heinous acts of violence against others during sexual encounters such as rape, not only alter their anger during the sexual act itself, but also depersonalize themselves from the victim altogether. Sometimes the end result can be death.

Like some of the violent men I've spoken to, serial killers separate themselves from reality and possess the ability to kill indiscriminately without feelings of empathy and remorse for their victims. As previously discussed, they usually have conflicts with reality as we see it or have illusions precipitated by fantasy. For example, we see a dead body as a human being and create our own story of how that person may or may have not suffered. Serial killers may see that same dead body as something entirely different and create their own story based on fantasy and delusions, minus empathy for the soul who once occupied the body.

Many types of sexually based killers who commit violent acts suffer from erectile dysfunctions and other sexual limitations. The fact that they suffer from sexual disorders drives their intense feelings of anger, hate and frustration further in the path of violent behavior. Hence, the long-standing, self-defeating knowledge of having a sexual limitation is not only "shameful" for any man to encounter during his lifetime, but it can be debilitating in establishing physical intimacy. Hence, it negatively impacts a man's view on himself and the relationship he forms with other human beings. One single event predisposed by unpleasant life experiences has been known to lure convicted killers into heinous acts of violence associated with the pain of past and present life circumstances. I will discuss the relevant aspects of this topic later in the following chapters.

Chapter I

SEXUAL FANTASY

Sexual fantasy is one of the hottest topics of discussion. It's also one of the premeditated motives behind the actions of most serial killers and rapists alike. Hence, this subject of intrigue is vastly distributed throughout the entire chapter in an attempt to understand the internal dynamics and motivational factors behind some of the most dangerous men ever to exist on American soil. Just sit back and read the stories and actively interpret some of the most inexplicable acts of violence.

Without the efforts of the Federal Bureau of Investigation, a branch of the US Department of Justice and the formation of the Behavioral Assessment Unit, the construct of this chapter would be null and void. From readings and research relevant to the topics of investigation and apprehension of serial killers, I've asked questions and developed theoretical constructs relevant to the techniques of the Federal Bureau of Investigation.

Before we springboard into a world of sexual fantasy from the eyes of a serial killer, I want you to put together pieces of a crime that involved a serial killer in captivity. The crime itself is viewed in a developmental perspective, with each clue leading to an inevitable event.

Once again, the perpetrator's fantasies are wishes establishing themselves in a developmental continuum. For example, a convicted rapist usually doesn't start out raping women. He has probably committed other petit crimes such as burglary, voyeuristic activities, assault and battery, or lewd and lascivious acts on a small child. Each and every one of these crimes can potentially escalate into more serious ones.

Even the process of murder is established in a step-by-step process. The element of a "surprise attack" is essential from a "sexual" perspective. In other words, how the victim responds to the surprise attack is necessary for the perpetrator to feel sexually aroused. I do mean sexually aroused in the broadest sense of the term.

Control must be established within the first sixty seconds of the attack for two reasons: Firstly, the killer's state of mind must be clear of conscious thought. Why? So that the fantasy can be brought to life. Secondly, the fantasy is brought to life both during and after the attack. Usually, if control cannot be established quickly, immediate death is the result. Why? Because the victim disrupts the perpetrator's routine as to the state of mind he's in before, during and after the attack.

For example, I interviewed an inmate who attacked his victim because he "wanted to see the color of her underwear". He couldn't establish control over the victim because she thought he was going to rape her. While the victim struggled, the perpetrator couldn't fulfill his fantasy (see her underwear) in a controlled manner.

Within seven minutes of massive strangulation the victim died of asphyxiation. In other words, the inmate I spoke to, choked her to death with his bare hands. The inmate did get to see her underwear and paid the ultimate price with his freedom. In this case, as in others, the perpetrator didn't intend to rape or physically harm this victim. Instead, the attacker intended to initiate control over his life. He also had an added fetish for women's undergarments. Reportedly, he'd been fantasizing about women's underwear for several years. His criminal history is somehow consistent with his wish and underwear fetish. For example, his prior arrests include a petty theft in which he stole a mannequin from a lingerie department, voyeuristic activities when he trespassed through a local high school and peeped inside a girl's bathroom, and burglary in an unoccupied dwelling. Guess what was stolen out of the house? Money, jewelry and women's underwear.

Finally, submission is the plateau phase of the attack. The sexual act is not as gratifying for the fantasy-based serial killer as is watching the victim lie, both terrified and helpless. When the victim is at the killer's mercy it's easy for him to humiliate and degrade her. In terms of the killer's thought process, it's the most gratifying point of the attack. Why? Because humiliation of the victim is one of the conscious motives of the fantasy-based serial killer. In most cases, the extent of the humiliation on the victim is indicative to the degree of humiliation the perpetrator feels and experiences for himself.

In almost all documented cases of serial killers they've experienced some type of childhood trauma or neglect that includes a base for humiliation.

Humiliating the victim is done in a variety of ways depending on the individual perpetrator. For example, many serial killers do not have intercourse with the victim, either because of a mental or physical ailment. However, one inmate I interviewed spat on his victim both pre- and post-mortem. A couple more inmates I interviewed have been known to insert foreign objects into their victim's vagina.

Humiliating the victim is all part of an endless process in establishing the ultimate unconscious wish, which is usually death for themselves and the victim.

Men who have extensive histories of violence tend to focus their thought processes and act on its behalf. Hence, they continue to alter their fate within the criminal justice system. Some men submit totally to their violent thought patterns and fantasies, creating a risk of permanence to their identity. If this happens it can be potentially dangerous for society because some of the men I've spoken with are at risk for further violent behavior. Some have been known to graduate to increased levels of severe violence.

The idea established in psychological thought, is the more severe and heinous the crime the more psychotic is the individual. However, this just means that the perpetrator harbors more resentment and anger towards his intended target. But the next question is, how do most serial killers and sex offenders obtain sexual gratification from the victims they choose?

The answer to this question is subjective depending on the individual. Before I begin, I want you to think about aspects of sexual intercourse. For the most part, sex to an anger-based rapist is energy directed as an outlet for the relief of physiological stressors and anger. For example, an object (penis) forcefully enters a woman's body (vagina). Once again, many of the sexual serial murderers and rapists are unable to obtain and maintain an erection. As a substitute they may use objects other than genitalia in entering the vagina. The device chosen fulfills the role of the penis in the wish to satisfy the victim. Inevitably, when this does not occur the perpetrator's "manhood" is challenged and he reacts violently towards the victim.

We'll later see the act of forcible rape leading to murder. The anger distributed in the act of rape stimulates and perhaps initiates further steps of violence, if not during the same time then later on during the course of the perpetrator's murder spree.

In most cases sex offenders and serial killers develop violent thought patterns during and throughout childhood. This process catapults itself from a particular incident into many instances of physical, sexual and emotional abuse by a mother, father, uncle, siblings and other authority figures.

Sexual serial killers are known to target women and children even if a male figure commits the abusive acts. Why? For obvious reasons. Women in general make an easier target. Another explanation is the source of anger and frustration of the perpetrator's inability to love others and maintain intimate relationships. For a less obvious reason I'll give you an example of an inmate I interviewed at Jackson Prison. He was sexually and physically abused by his father while his mother stood and watched. In this case, the inmate's father committed the acts of physical and sexual abuse. As a result, the inmate became angry at his mother for ignoring what the father continued to do at his expense. In the inmate's mind his mother perpetuated and enabled the abuse. He blamed her for not feeling his pain. This inmate is serving a life sentence for two counts of murder against a prostitute and her unborn child. He beat the prostitute so badly that she will spend the rest of her life in a coma. As a result of being kicked repeatedly in the abdomen, the prostitute lost her seven-month unborn fetus. This woman will never again walk, talk, eat, or breathe the air on her own because she owed a man fifty dollars.

Early in October 1986, inmate X attacked, raped and murdered a middle-aged woman watching television at her residence in Cleveland, Ohio. He broke into her apartment, raped her and stabbed her eighty-two times. He fled the scene two hours later, leaving her naked. He also took fifteen pictures of her mutilated body. Nothing was removed from the house and the victim was fondled pre- and post-mortem. Inmate X would be classified as a modern-day, anger-based sex offender who possesses the character-logical traits of a would-be serial killer.

Fortunately, authorities were able to apprehend inmate X before he had the opportunity to kill or rape again. Judging by his lack of remorse and empathy for his victim and her family, exuberated sexual satisfaction from the act itself, grandiose behavior, and the brutality of the crime itself, it's likely this man would commit future violence if given the opportunity. But who are we to predict a future violence such as homicide? I wish I had a crystal ball in front of me telling the tales of the future; unfortunately this is never the case.

Sex offenders, such as anger-based rapists, primarily act out their anger and pre-morbid sexual desire towards small children and women. Once again, anger is primarily expressed in the form of sexual intercourse, and orgasm occurs on witnessing the struggle of the victim. Small children are easy to control and the real young ones (two and three-year-olds) are too young to understand what's happening. Sexual intercourse and the creation of fantasy are subjective for each attacker. In other words, the perpetrator's penis doesn't necessarily have to penetrate the vagina to achieve orgasm. Instead, a universally based resolution is established by the perpetrator once his victim comes under complete control. The resolution is established as a result of the perpetrator's heightened sexual experience with the child. And whatever it is, he'll continue to find the means to satisfy his insatiable appetite.

Chapter II
UNPREDICTABILITY

Serial killers are known to be the most dangerous perpetrators, usually as a result of their unpredictable thought patterns, as to where, when, who, and how they're going to strike. Hence, their motive and method of operation significantly alter local and state police investigation. They're usually opportunistic individuals who look for weaknesses in their potential prey just as lions look for a weak antelope. Sometimes the only remorse the serial killer has for himself is the fact he was caught and that he may never have the opportunity to kill again.

I remember a man in D–block told me he had sliced a beautiful woman's throat and had sex with her while she bled to death. Another man tied a woman to a bedpost and kept biting her neck until he ruptured a major artery. How does a man get to this point and enjoy it? The thoughts that come to mind are vampire movies or sadism. Both are interchangeable and rely on different methods of fulfillment. For example, in the movies, vampires are more methodical, mysterious, cold and callous, whereas sadism involves the totality of pairing sex with violence and humiliating the partner.

Sadistic action, or the popular term "sadism" is sexually gratifying for most of the violent men I interview on a daily basis. I've also interviewed an inmate who attempted to drink the blood of his cat. In previous sessions he revealed he used to have sex with animals. Vampirism and sadism are primarily motivated by sexual fantasies.

Human beings have come long and far in the evolutionary process. Yet we remain internally attached to some of our primitive instincts. According to Freud, relative concepts of sex and aggression were thought to go hand in hand. His thoughts and beliefs held true throughout the nineteenth century and will probably continue during the next millennium.

If you process sex and aggression in the relative sense of having sexual intercourse, then Freud was right. Let's think about having sex for a moment. When you hear a woman scream or breathe rather loudly in your ear, doesn't that excite some people? Or, do you find yourself being aroused primarily at this level?

Some of the violent men convicted of rape, tune sensorily into the same thing, but on a more escalated and sadistic level. A few of the men I've spoken to are willing to go a step further to obtain the level of satisfaction in order to reach orgasm, perhaps even accidentally killing their victim in the process.

What does it mean to behave psychotically? Before we get to that point, first let's talk about what it means to be abnormal in an unpredictable and nonconformist sense? Most people generalize abnormality as simply going against the grain as society dictates. For example, if I were to run around naked on a crowded street in broad daylight, people would view my behavior as abnormal as well as unpredictable. Our society believes a normal day consists of waking up at a reasonable hour, getting dressed, wearing shoes, going to work, coming home, eating dinner, and so on. It's considered abnormal to sleep until 4:00 P.M. every day, wear slippers to a construction site, drink beer for lunch, and eat dinner in your bathtub. These types of behavior seem pretty abnormal, don't they?

This may seem abnormal to you and I put to someone who lives the lifestyle feels and believes they are behaving quite normally. The same applies to the thought process of a serial killer. For example, killing becomes a daily routine that relieves him of pain and stress. Hence, killing is rationalized in a context of normalcy because it allows him to function in the world. Remember, we need to think about what abnormality really is, and not become blinded by clinical diagnoses.

Basically, abnormality is an advent of behavior inconsistent with the norms of society. Hence, behaving "normally" is the most effective shield against subjecting ourselves to shame and humiliation.

So the next question is, are we abnormal if we possess violent thought patterns relevant to sexual desire? I would say "no" psychically and "yes" to character traits that are either relevant or irrelevant to our ideal personality and ideology. For example, say a person has sexual fantasies pertaining to the destruction of human body parts, or believes in slicing a person's throat in the heat of anger, or they have fantasies of being raped. If that person behaves consistently with these thought processes then he or she is deemed as behaving rather abnormally. For instance, if a man or a woman has fantasies including rape and the destruction of body parts facilitating sexual arousal, then he or she is not completely abnormal in the sense of the word. However, if they voluntarily slice a woman's leg to initiate a sexual fantasy, it's safe to say that their behavior is indeed abnormal. In some cases we can go a step further and categorize any behavior as psychotic.

Don't get me wrong: having abnormal thoughts and fantasies about sexual fulfillment is not abnormal. However, behaving in a consistent manner with these thoughts and sexual fantasies would be considered abnormal. It's not every day that people go out looking to be raped by a stranger, or a person takes a trip to the morgue in the middle of the day asking for body parts in order to masturbate.

Consistently acting on behalf of abnormal thoughts can and eventually will subject us to madness. The reason for this is that it disrupts the balance of ideal thinking that was forced on us as a direct result of interacting and being a part of a system.

There are only a few thoughts invited to bypass our system enabling us to exist inside the boundaries of our true self. The more we continue to deviate from our system the more pathological we inevitably become. Why? Because deviation sets up isolation. Hence, love and respect for yourself and others become more ambivalent and difficult to embrace.

Thoughts that are transformed into behavior are determined by our societal code. This code is instilled upon us throughout our development. We transfer thoughts into expression because they are acceptable to the society in which we live. The thoughts society rejects and we embrace are automatically repressed within our unconscious brain. Our brain serves as the gatekeeper in letting any foreign material and repressed conflicts back into our conscious repertoire. If the gatekeeper is functioning abnormally then unwanted memories, conflicts and fantasies enter conscious thought. If one fantasy is let through then it can start an unhealthy chain reaction of internal conflict. If the unwanted side of our personality is expressive then it can negatively affect all other facets of daily activity. As a result, we may experience cognitive disequilibrium. Once this unbalance occurs, we find it difficult to exist within our system because we ignore, or can no longer distinguish between appropriate and inappropriate behavior.

The initial imbalance in thinking creates internal conflict, thus predisposing us to insanity. Initial stages of insanity can occur when one part of our mind is in conflict with the other. As such, when you are unable to establish equilibrium between your two selves they divide into four parts, hence creating even more indecisive behavior in decision-making skills. From this point on, you begin to question how yourself and everyone else around you exist. The trust in yourself and others diminishes until you feel that a part of your inner self has died. When the uncertainty of your environment and system predominates your subconscious thoughts, your psyche splinters off even further until you have difficulty in processing "right" from "wrong". Morals established by parents and society rapidly dissipate into the dimensions of forgetfulness.

The more your conscious mind splits off, the more distant you become from your true self and your inability to obtain equilibrium. Now that your psyche has splintered into so many different directions it becomes virtually impossible for you to remain a balanced person.

Insanity occurs when the splitting mind creates deception in our thinking processes. As such, violent men are not insane due to their impulsivity but act impulsively due to their insanity.

Relative to this discussion, psychologically bipolar disorder and borderline personality disorder result from a process of unpredictable behavior and mind splitting. Bipolar depression occurs as a result of feeling helpless because the mind has not established an appropriate balance. One inmate I interviewed in prison, who happened to be diagnosed with bipolar disorder, couldn't decide whether to kill himself or rob a bank! Both behaviors represent a desperate attempt for this man to establish balance and control in his life. This man described his world as being cold and dark because he never found direction in his life. In his case mania occurred as a defense mechanism (reaction formation) against his overwhelming feelings of fear and anxiety. Hence, this can occur as a result of the mind splitting into several directions, creating more confusion and chaos. Violence can inevitably occur as a result of uncontrolled mind splitting and elated points of mania.

The victims of serial killers fall into several groups classified by age, race, sex, economic and social hierarchy. How do these victims get chosen and why? Is it a case of being in the wrong place at the wrong time? Or, does the killer choose his victim in accordance with the selection process mediated by his internal thought processes?

In penetrating the surface of these questions we must first assess the killer's level of functioning before, during and after the crime itself. Hence, we must understand his motivational process as to the victim he chooses. We can perhaps accomplish this by examining the killer's unconscious thought process before, during and after the crime itself. We must examine the process by including sexual fantasy as one of his primary driven forces. For example, how does his fantasy relate to the victims he has selected time and again?

What is a serial killer's level of functioning before, during and after his crime? What are his reactions to the violence and bloodshed he causes? Before the crime occurs our first impressions of serial killers usually come straight from the media. Most movies, newspapers, and journals portray the serial killer as a clean-cut, middle-aged gentleman, a smooth-talker, who is pleasant and a mild-mannered man from the outside, with noticeable intellectual prowess. For the most part, this stereotype is typically false. In some cases serial killers fit this description. However, many suffer from some type of mental illness. His abilities to function like you and I slowly deteriorate. Hence, sometimes his odd behavior is so noticeable that you're able to spot him and people like him in a crowded place.

The individual's appearance and behavior provide clues into whether or not our perpetrator is functioning normally. Of course, my definition of normal may be different from my readers. My definition is rather simplistic. Normally, it is merely certain behavioral traits that remain consistent with the norms in a given context. Hence, any behavior that is against the norm outside of this context is considered abnormal. Examples of abnormal behavior in a serial killer cannot be seen only in his actions but in his thought process and appearance as well. He can be disorganized and intoxicated. For example, he talks to strangers and asks them strange and unruly questions that are displaced and out of the context of reality. He has a rather disheveled appearance, his hair is a mess, and his pattern of speech is discombobulated. Hence, he probably has a learning disorder – aphasia, or some kind of learning or communication difficulties. Additionally, this type of serial killer is likely to be suffering from an aforementioned mental illness, such as paranoid schizophrenia. The symptoms created from a serious thought disorder like schizophrenia, applied to a violent man, can progress to a point where killing is the only justified means to his survival. Hence, unconscious thoughts regarding both death and destruction are expressed through the killer's emotional pain of existing in the present.

The type of serial killer mentioned above is not as selective in choosing his victim to fulfill his sexual fantasy. This type of killer, like others, is opportunistic. Hence, he'll kill anyone in the same geographical region. For example, killers who are mentally ill usually hunt within their own geographical region. Their choice of victim is contingent on their own paranoid thought process. Within his mind the act of murder is an unconscious wish sometimes triggered by paranoid thoughts, delusions and/or hallucinations.

What about the killers who don't suffer from any known mental illness categorized by the DIAGNOSTIC AND STATISTICAL MANUAL OF MENTAL DISORDERS (FOURTH EDITION) (DSM-IV)? For example, on the outside these guys appear to be completely normal. This type of serial killer is the most ruthless because his existence is identical to his prey, except it's predicated on willful acts of violence against individuals completely unknown to him. This fact alone makes him very difficult to catch. The only weakness he possesses, is in the fact that killing is a psychological addiction. Hence, the impulse to kill is uncontrollable because it bears much relief and gives an emotional and physical high.

Serial killers don't necessarily become addicted to the act of violence as opposed to the rush created from the victim's facial expressions. To enhance their psychological functioning manifested by their sexual fantasies, serial killers will continue to commit violent acts against others. Murder is needed to fulfill sexual fantasies of power and control. We will continue to talk extensively about this topic in upcoming chapters.

Those who kill for sport become addicted to the risk of getting caught. In other words, they want to see if they can get away with the crime for as long as they can. Some serial killers and serial rapists are known to hang out at cop bars just to get information, or wallow in the chance of hearing the police discuss their crime spree. This gives them an overblown sense of accomplishment and self worth.

To understand the addiction process, compare a serial killer to an addicted gambler. Addictive gamblers keep playing, even if they're losing. As with serial killers, winning is a secondary gain to their addiction. Instead, the primary gain is the thrill of putting everything on the line. It's the moment before we realize if the hand is a winner or loser. The serial killer's game and measurement of thrill is the success or failure of getting away with the kill, not to mention the fact he has complete control over another human being's life. The difference between a gambler and a serial killer is that the serial killer derives pleasure from being in control while the gambler relinquishes control to the dealer. The serial killer comes up a winner each time he leaves the table with another victim dead. However, both the gambler and the serial killer will be back to play another hand until one gets caught, or, in the gambler's case, loses his money.

Methodical serial killers, as I'd like to call them, carefully gauge their victim, plan their attack and chalk out the disposal of the victim's body. They usually have average to above-average intelligence. Hence, Roy Hazelwood of the FBI refers to these types of serial killers as organized offenders. Again, organized offenders are usually selective in choosing their victims, and are somewhat intelligent because they've managed to evade authorities for long periods of time. They're cautious in planning out their attack and getting rid of the body. These killers consider every move carefully and usually don't leave physical evidence at the scene that might implicate them to the crime. They approach adverse situations with the utmost confidence. Some of these dangerous predators are known to possess antisocial personality traits. However, inability to notice them on the surface makes these guys even more lethal. For example, one of the more dangerous weapons these guys have in luring their victims into potential harm is the use of manipulative tactics in tricking the potential victim into trusting them. For example, you've seen this method of luring with Ted Bundy. Ted's manipulative mindset existed at the surface of his psyche. Hence, that was what made it easy for him to effectively play the role of a nice guy. Organized offenders like Ted Bundy usually consider the end result of violence as an art form. For example, collecting souvenirs, pictures, and body parts from their victims reminds them of their successful attack and subsequent murder.

Most organized offenders, according to Hazelwood, lead rather private lives. They're usually never satisfied with their lives and never have found anything they were really good at. Hence, there really isn't much that makes them feel proud. Committing the ultimate crime of murder has temporarily put them in the limelight of success, a feeling not often felt. They succeeded at pulling off something very difficult that gives them the attention they've always wanted.

Most human beings possess a variety of protective shields. I refer to these shields as belonging to something or someone, getting attention, accomplishments, goals and feeling proud as a result of sustaining your protective shields. For example, being proud of doing well in school, belonging to a fraternity, a religious affiliation, family bonds, and generally feeling good about yourself. Often, these shields protect us from wandering off the path of passivity into the realm of violence.

Chapter III
FOUNTAIN OF YOUTH

When a serial killer plans to kidnap, rape and murder a child, his motive is usually stealing the innocence often associated with children. I'll get back to this in a while. First, why would a serial killer choose a small child over an adult? An obvious answer is that a child is easier to handle and physically take control of. The not so obvious answer is that a child is used to fulfill some sort of sexual fantasy.

A possible link to the answer of why a serial killer chooses a child possibly reflects upon the era of Darwinism. Charles Darwin talked about the term infanticide. This is when social species of animals kill off infants in order to eliminate their competitors' gene pool. This is common in wolf packs. A male wolf will kill its competitors' gene pool for two reasons. One, so the female can ovulate: she is unable to get pregnant while nursing infants. Two, instinctually the wolf would want to implant its gene within the pack. Hence, this concept may occur at an unconscious level with violent men who select children as victims. Think about it! When you hear of a violent man being a victim of violence himself it usually occurs from a stepparent during their younger years of life. Hence, parents from the same gene pool are a lot less likely to kill off or harm their own kind.

The same philosophical reasoning exists regarding anger and aggression. When anger and aggression dominate the psyche we rarely kill off our own species. Animals, as opposed to humans, have a hypothetical turn-off switch when anger and aggression dominate their psyche. You can visualize this turn-off switch in animal behavior. For example, when two animals of the same species are fighting it's very rare that one will kill the other; the reason being that one of the animals usually submits. Submission is the mechanism that turns off this hypothetical switch. Humans who do not have this mechanism or turn-off switch, such as serial killers, react violently against members of their own species. The use of deadly weapons allows us to express our anger towards others in a relatively safe manner to ourselves, and this is why we possess increased levels of intra-psychic aggression within the same species of the human race.

Perhaps, one of the defense tactics for an individual confronted by a serial killer or sexual predator is falling into a defenseless or submissive posture. I wouldn't advise this. However, if you think about it we use submission as a defense tactic every day. For example, when couples argue one will eventually give up and that will be the end of that. In a hypo-thetical situation, if we were abducted by a sexual predator, submissive tactics could possibly diminish the thrill of the attack. However, could this induce more extreme violent behavior? For instance, if the attacker finds pleasure in inflicting pain on his victim (sadism) then sexual pleasure forms at the surface of his victim's struggle. When the victim subdues herself in a defensive posture the struggle no longer facilitates his sexual fantasy. Therefore, the attacker must justify another means of attaining sexual gratification. Hence, that's when he may become violent.

Are all violent men recipients of violence and abuse themselves? Not necessarily. However, I would say that most have at the very least witnessed some violence, if not being directly involved in it. Abuse occurs at different spectrums in one's life. For example, it can occur during childhood and adulthood and the experience doesn't have to be limited to forms of violence. For example, the individual can experience emotional pain through difficulties in relating to others in the past and present, particularly in the case of violent men who've had difficulties with the opposite sex. Hence, serial killers, who usually target women, have difficulties establishing relationships with the opposite sex during adolescence, which often continues into early adulthood. This perhaps provides one explanation of why some violent sociopaths possess homosexual tendencies. This statement is speculative, but requires thinking. Don't you think a person who behaves out of the norm, especially a small child, will have difficulties attracting others from the opposite sex? Middle school and high school can be very damaging to young kids who are ridiculed. For example, think of that one person in high school who attracts the most negative attention, either physically or as a result of strange behavior. Think of that one person in your class whom people identified as a loser. There's always a student who acts different from the rest of the classmates, and usually he or she becomes the target of ridicule. As we have recently seen in public schools, ridicule can be a motivational cue for extreme cases of violence, as with Columbine High School.

It's important for a male child to sustain a healthy relationship with both of his parents. The mother is most important in sustaining physical and emotional well-being and the father is most important in establishing social well-being. During adolescence your peers have just as much influence on your social well-being as your father does. I'm not suggesting that all violent men who commit violent acts against women experience extreme difficulty in forming relationships with them. I'm merely suggesting that a male sociopath may select a pretty young girl in a particular age range for several different reasons, and one of those may be his previous absence of popularity. The killer who stalks young girls isn't as discriminating of their age – as long as they look young and beautiful it's okay. Perhaps in the killer's mind there's no way he'll ever see himself together with a pretty young girl. So in order to fulfill his fantasy he must capture and control her. Otherwise she wouldn't have anything to do with him.

In a sense, the soul of the female victim fills a void in the killer's life. This void is unknown, perhaps even unknown to the killer himself. By holding his female victim hostage he finally has what he's always wanted… respect and dignity.

As noted earlier, it's rather difficult to advise a female who is abducted by a violent sociopath on how to act. Some experts say that relaxing calms the aggressor down. However, if you're dealing with an attacker with different motives this approach can also be fatal.

There have been instances where the female victim expresses fear and the serial killer becomes sexually stimulated. In this case the killer uses his victim's fear to facilitate his sexual fantasy.

If you're abducted by a serial killer the end result is usually death. Whether or not it's a quick death depends on the role the victim plays in his fantasy.

Most human beings, whether they're suffering from mental or psychiatric illness, or are in a violent state of mind, possess a complementary passive state that can be reached at any given moment.

Serial killers possess a passive state of mind but usually choose to ignore it. Hence, in doing so, they ignore their victim's pleas, tears, and the tone of their voice. The serial killer usually ignores auditory effects. However, he relies primarily on vision. With this in mind non-verbal visibility can possibly initiate a serial killer's passive state of mind.

The best method to avoid being chosen as a victim is avoiding dangerous situations that make you vulnerable. For example, kids who walk to school alone take shortcuts down rural roads and sidewalks, and those who alienate themselves from the other children, make good targets.

Chapter IV
DAWN OF TODAY

We've talked about killers being influenced by their parents and peers in the past. But what about the killers who are influenced as a result of the present? These types of killers perceive themselves as casualties of the environment. Some of these violent men come from decent families, and have been raised in average to above-average economic backgrounds. Some theorists believe that society wraps its tentacles around them and strengthens their impulse to kill. By society, I'm referring to the culture and norms that govern a broad demographic area.

The United States has a growing problem and that is the increasing number of violent criminals. If you are in any type of law enforcement, you can expect to see a lot more violence in the years to come. The reasons seem almost obvious when I explain them.

Research shows that the prison population in the US has increased almost eighty per cent since 1994. Our country spends more dollars on prisons than it does on education alone. In twelve states, including Florida, prosecutors use their discretion in prosecuting children as young as thirteen as adults. Our country is developing a philosophy: "Lock 'em up and throw away the key." For some people, this concept is very enticing. Why not lock them all up and keep them caged? The fact of the matter is that eventually their prison term will end. The next question we ask is, are they rehabilitated? Unfortunately, for the most part, not in the way in which we as a society can feel comfortable and sleep at night. Those in the thirteen to twenty-four age range will probably be more violent after they're released from prison! Prison teaches you to become violent and to think like a criminal. Prisoners have to be manipulative, and sometimes violent in order to survive.

Seemingly, violent crime is curbed to the credit of law enforcement agencies. However, how long will this remain? Some of the incarcerated violent men will be released from prison soon. We have to hold ourselves accountable for the product that prisons produce.

America is the only country in the world that glorifies violence in the media so much. Think about the movies and what we see on TV. I remember when I was ten years old I couldn't catch anything on TV that was violent past 11:00 P.M. Just the other day, they were showing a movie on TV at 8:00 P.M. called *An Eye for an Eye*. In the beginning of the movie a fifteen-year-old girl is brutally raped and murdered. Children view such violence every day on television because violent programs are viewed during prime-time hours.

Today, movie producers are making more money off violent movies than romance and comedy put together. The movies and media alike encourage men to show off their masculinity through committing violent acts against others. Think about it! What fun would a movie be if the star just talked himself out of violence the entire course of the movie? Most of us wouldn't sit through a movie if there wasn't at least some sex or violence. Media isn't the only thing that contributes to violence.

Today, we live in a world of computer technology. Innovative technologies and advancements approach humankind, at a pace which is faster than ever before. What does this have to do with producing a violent sociopath? For starters, the use of computers and other technologies takes away some of our humanness. Instead of expressing ourselves through each other we tend to do it through the use of computers. Advancements and innovations can produce more jobs but they take away the important ones. All of these concepts increase the amount of competition in our society to an absolute maximum. As a result of this intense competition we no longer see humans as good, helpful and loving. Instead, we see each other as cold and getting in the way of our dreams. These feelings cause everyone to tense up and project a defensive posture on human contact. As a result, a negative aura forms around others and across the world, especially those in big cities and metropolitan areas. People in large cities are usually perceived to be out for themselves.

When we look at people in a cold and negative light we can form pathological impulses of violence towards them. Indeed some of these impulses can reach the outer limits of extreme violence. When you have reached your limit it takes one act or situation to set you over the edge, and perhaps into a violent rage – for example, if you get a D in a class, you lose your job, or you lose everything in the stock market. Although these things can be negative, they're not strong enough alone to throw you off the edge. They could cause you to break down emotionally, but there has to be another element to cause you to kill another human being. There must be a pathological impulse to kill before the final trigger of violence takes effect. The impulse may come from over-competitiveness in society and our reactions to it. The final trigger can be anything that sets you off the edge into the realm of madness.

The mass murderer is a prime candidate to fall into the previous theoretical concept. It usually takes only one instance or stressor that drives the passion to kill within us. This instance, or these instances, can cause a person to act impulsively and irrationally.

Mass murderers are completely different from the methodical serial killer in that their reason for murder is completely null and void. The serial killer is functional and somewhat rational when committing his crime. The mass murderer is completely irrational; for example, his crime, motive and act of violence show this. For instance, a man walks in to a post office and shoots everyone working on that day; or a man strolls in to a McDonalds and blasts up the place.

These are relatively desperate men living desperate lives, who commit desperate acts. They cling on to their own lives by justifying the deaths of innocent people in an attempt to gain some of the control that was originally lost in their lives. Unfortunately, it's very rare to capture a mass murderer alive. Unfortunately, they usually turn the gun on themselves, or they are killed by law enforcement officers who, by duty, try to protect themselves and others.

The serial killer is less predictable regarding his moves, motive and choice of victim. The mass murderer is less predictable in regard to his criminal behavior. Both the serial killer and mass murderer attempt to establish some sense of control in their lives. However, control for the mass murderer exists more through his reality. Hence, control for the serial killer exists more through his fantasy. The mass murderer's motive is usually about revenge and control created from feelings of hopelessness and anger. The serial killer's motive is usually facilitated by sexual impulses that manifest themselves through wishes, dreams, fantasies of power, revenge and self-control.

Chapter V

THE TRAINED KILLER

Usually as adults we're programmed to control our anger and hostility. However, as children we're limited in this respect. For instance, when a child is beaten, neglected and abused he is programmed, in respect of the term, to repeat the same behavior in the future through observational learning.

I'll give you another example for someone who is an adult. A twenty-seven-year-old male I had once met in prison indicated he had a personal grudge towards women. While talking to him I realized his deliberate hostility towards women. After speaking with this individual for a while, he told me a story about how his father paid for him to have sex with a prostitute on his eighteenth birthday. This person I'm speaking about never had any previous sexual contact with a woman. Next, he described his first ever-sexual encounter with this prostitute. He quotes, "She asked me to tie her up to the bedpost. She wanted me to get a whip and hit her on the stomach with it." He adds, "I thought this was a bit odd but I enjoyed it very much. I particularly enjoyed when she let me whip her stomach and bite on her inner thigh. I did have trouble getting an erection, but she was patient."

Now at the age of twenty-seven, this young man is serving six life sentences for the brutal murders of six prostitutes which occurred in less than eight months. Cause of death was usually asphyxiation. However, almost all the victims had their stomachs slit across the middle (post-mortem). If not strangled to death his victims were knocked unconscious by a blunt object. As a result, he was able to fulfill his ritualistic fantasies that inevitably resulted in murder. Whether or not these killings tie into the perpetrator's first sexual encounter with a prostitute is a mystery.

If you recall, this young man's first sexual encounter with a prostitute occurred with a negative twist. Hence, he received sexual satisfaction through the act of degrading another human being. Perhaps as an indirect result of this experience he viewed the female gender in a negative light. For example, his perceptions of women can vary from being incapable of love to incapable of trust. This example is not to say that all young men who've experienced sexual contact with a prostitute will inherit the same thought process. However, this particular individual has had additional difficulties adjusting to the emotional aspects of sustaining a relationship with the opposite sex. Hence, throughout his life he's had difficulties pleasing women on both a physical and emotional level. Can the reasons be attributed to his first sexual encounter? Of course, his one sexual experience alone doesn't initiate violence against women. His thought processes managed to follow him through the years as a result of this experience and perhaps others like it. The fact of the matter is that this person enjoyed harming the prostitute when he was eighteen years old. Hence, at the age of twenty-seven, his fantasies remain consistent with the sexual acts performed on the prostitute when he was eighteen. For that one moment his behavior was encouraged by his role model (his father). Hence, he was given permission to relive his sexual fantasies that would have remained dormant for years.

As time passed he was angry because many of the women he was acquainted with, and desired to have sexual relations with, were not willing to conform to his sadistic fantasies. For almost ten years this young man continued to seek out prostitutes in order to relive his sadistic sexual fantasies. The fantasies progressed from slapping to punching. Hence, he found himself paying money to a prostitute to pretend she was being raped. Soon he didn't pay for it anymore. Finally, his sadistic behavior graduated to murder. Even though his first murder was an accident he went on and continued to experience his fantasies by killing more prostitutes.

As this young man continued to seek out prostitutes, feelings of shame and inadequacy consumed his soul. For example, at eighteen years of age he was aroused when the prostitute cried and moaned in pain. His shameful feelings became mixed with an inner sexual desire that allowed him to kill more prostitutes. To him they were nothing but pieces of meat responsible for making him feel ashamed of himself. They were also responsible for providing him with sexual pleasure.

As a young adult his lack of understanding towards women decreased even further. He couldn't figure out why women didn't want anything to do with him intimately and why he had to pay for it. He considered himself an average-looking young man with a charming personality. In the beginning he attempted to please his sexual partners just as he did the prostitute. Unfortunately, he discovered, after being rejected by females, that he was going about it all wrong. As each rejection took place, new forms of hatred began to creep in to this young man's already debilitating ego. Anger and hate consumed daily life functioning. As he grew older this young man realized one of the worst things that could've possibly put him over the edge. He understood that the prostitute was faking her sexual excitement when he was eighteen. As a young man he not only felt shame and rejection, but he could not trust women at all. Hence, he perceived romantic love and sexual pleasure as deceit.

Now at twenty-seven, this convicted serial killer views sex as a violent construct, created out of his own feelings of shame, rejection and his perceptions of deceit. Hence, sexual contacts with women project his feelings of shame and anger on to them. The killer avenges his past and present experiences of rejection and betrayal. Hence, having sex with prostitutes allows him to release this negative energy, if you will call it that, in a safe environment with minimal distractions.

Each sexual encounter bares feelings of shamefulness and inadequacy. As a result, his anger and frustration soak through the pores of his skin, leaving his search for manhood in the midst of violence. His every move to relieve one of man's worst enemies – "shame" – is blanketed by thoughts of harming the prostitutes. This individual believes the only way to reach orgasm is to relive the identical scenes related to his fantasies. As a result, not only will the killer be sexually satisfied, but he also temporarily eliminates the psychological pain associated with fear and rejection.

Some serial killers are known to relive the event through masturbating. When this individual masturbates to violence he increases his negative images towards women. These negative images grow stronger each time the fantasy is relived through the realities of being rejected or betrayed by a member of the same or opposite sex. The reality of rejection is recorded in the perpetrator's brain and is played over and over again, during the course of masturbation.

Over the course of time, masturbating to violent material causes the perpetrator to habitually excite himself through the pain he projects onto his masturbating material. Hence, the perpetrator will perceive sex and emotion as pain that may end up in violence. Feelings of hate, betrayal and shame mixed with the sexual desire for pain and mutilation, are the focal points of motivation.

Chapter VI
THE MAKING OF A SERIAL KILLER

The kids I interview on a daily basis are the kids society generally wants to throw out. Eventually, most of these kids will end up dead or behind bars. The adolescents I speak with and subsequently used to defend, exhibit poor impulse control and were usually diagnosed with dysthymia, major depressive episodes, learning disorder, reading disorder and conduct disorder.

Some of these kids immediately act on their impulses rather than express what they're feeling in an intense situation. Their feelings are repressed by the socio-cultural structure from which they continue to be exposed. They have difficulty expressing emotions because expressiveness is noted as a sign of weakness by most of their peers. Those who have the slightest presumption of being mentally challenged, their first instinct is protecting themselves by sheltering their emotions. Instead, they learn to shield off their feelings and react violently as a means of escaping feelings of isolation, inadequacy, sadness and pain. Most of these kids lack a positive support system inviting them to express their feelings. Many of these adolescents choose not to feel hurt, desire and guilt because of the pain it produces within. They choose not to experience these emotions because they've learned stereotypical behavior of how men and women should act. They don't want to be thought of as a "punk" or a "sell out" on the street. Some of these thoughts can precipitate into violence. However, most of the adolescents are not violent.

Most of the adolescents I speak to bottle up their emotions inside, and are waiting to explode at the slightest provocation.

Hence, some factors of potential serial killers are symptoms of frustration created from years of repressed painful thoughts and emotions. Add this to their current economic/environmental stressors and their predisposition to violence increases tenfold.

Some of the adolescents I speak with subconsciously intellectualize with their ego. Hence, they tell themselves to feel and act the opposite of what their pain and guilt produce within. For example, instead of taking out their anger and frustration on the person who's abusing them, their negative energy is displaced on another living object, perhaps an easier or more vulnerable target and even themselves.

Usually a perpetrator who expresses emotional pain will attack a victim that best represents the pain he or she feels. His attack and choice of victim depends on who is the most vulnerable. For example, a case I received was indicative of this. An eighteen-year-old adolescent male raped a ten-year-old boy. The eighteen-year-old had been raped by his father, when he was only nine years old. During the eighteen-year-old's sexual encounter with the ten-year-old victim he expressed feelings of anger, resentment and excitement over the illicit act. In this case the sexual act wasn't about love, desire and a sexual passion for the boy. Instead, the sexual act was about lust, hatred and rage for what happened to him as a child, and it was being expressed sexually. Unconsciously the perpetrator is guilty for what happened to him as a child. Thus, because he was raped by his father he was never able to develop age-appropriate sexual maturity. His current sexual advancements towards young children displayed guilt and anger for what had previously occurred in his life. The perpetrator deals with anger, frustration and guilt by transforming himself into the aggressor. This is one way to establish control. You're not looking at an eighteen-year-old young man; instead you're looking at an eighteen-year-old boy functioning like a nine-year-old.

In some of the juvenile sexual offenders I interview, rage is an established response facilitated by an environmental and genetic component, which we will discuss later.

In young, violent sexual offenders, rage is created from repressed anger and aggression and is facilitated within the domain of both fear and fantasy. It remains dormant in their subconscious until something in the environment triggers its response. These so-called triggers can be anything from simple to more complex stimuli in the environment. They are usually sexual in nature. They can be deployed and lead an alcoholic to drink again. For example, you're a heterosexual male rapist at a party where women occupy the scene. A simple stimulus such as perfume and its aroma can stimulate a physiological response for the rapist to attack.

Again, most of the adolescents I interview experience anger and frustration as a result of post-traumatic events that have taken place at some point in their lives. Hence, as a result it cripples their already debilitating egos. Usually these adolescents do not have the mental, or even intellectual capacity to cope with extreme traumatic events, such as witnessing violence or being stabbed and shot. Some of these factors can lead to violent crime.

Adolescents who witness or suffer severe physical abuse need to feel a sense of belonging, which is important in empowering their own sense of positive self-worth. When children and adolescents are physically and severely emotionally abused and their egos are being attacked, in some cases they end up severely crippled.

During the initial stages of some adolescents committing violent crime they're often persuaded by friends, relatives, authority figures or significant others. For example, a child may observe an older friend, a role model, a parent, commit violent acts against others. If they continue to commit petty crimes these kids may eventually go on to commit worse crimes against humanity.

Some kids figure they're able to get away with it the first time so why not try it again? Some really don't understand or respect the law enough to listen to a first, second, or third warning. Each time an adolescent breaks the law he or she gets slapped on the wrist, and they are told not to do it again. Finally, when they commit a similar, or even a more serious crime the prosecutor decides to charge them as adults. Unfortunately, this has not worked in deterring violent juvenile crime.

Today, pressure from society and state legislatures forces prosecutors to impose adult sanctions on children. All this provides is a band-aid for a wound that eventually will become infected. The circuit court judges adhere to the written laws of the constitution, and if by chance justice is served then so is humanity in the long run.

Chapter VII

PARADIGMS OF A SERIAL KILLER

One of the reasons a serial killer develops a genuine taste for killing is the risk associated with getting caught. Unfortunately, the more victims they kill the more efficient they become. However, someday they'll make a careless error which will inevitably get them caught. Part of their thrill is creating a cat and mouse game for authorities.

The older a serial killer, the more difficult it is for him to conform to a life of good. This is not to say they can never change. However, it's very difficult for them to change because most of their violent behavior was initiated as part of an addictive process. For example, it's very difficult to change the behavior of sexual offenders, such as pedophiles. The reason is that you're attempting to change their overall sexual orientation, what and who they feel comfortable with. For example, you're a heterosexual male and someone is trying to rehabilitate you to be a homosexual. The only part of sexuality you can change is becoming abstinent. This is exactly how most sexual offenders successfully rehabilitate themselves when released from incarceration. Sexual offender recidivism depends on each situation they encounter, as well as individual strength.

When you enter the stages of rape and murder, it becomes increasingly difficult to change your pattern of violent behavior because the crime itself serves as a form of relief to the perpetrator. For example, most serial killers need to express themselves and what they are feeling by killing another human being. Hence, their usual selective killing relieves both psychological and physiological stress.

A serial killer by definition is an efficient killer who may or may not develop his skills over time. The serial killer attempts to establish a positive identity by successfully killing his prey, and in the process he masks his true identity. His identity can be revealed in the mess he leaves behind.

Most of the juveniles charged with sexual battery and rape, have themselves been sexually abused by a parent or a relative. Approximately ninety per cent of juveniles, who kill their parents, were abused themselves. How does this happen? A learned pattern of behavior continues to exist for these troubled youths. For example, if within your existence you've experienced physical, sexual and emotional abuse by a significant other, the chances of you repeating that behavior, either directly or indirectly, are very high.

Instead of throwing out an easy explanation to the previous statement, I will present it in a live situation. I want you to imagine being raped by your father, brother and/or uncle. During the instance of you being the victim attacked you don't know how to feel. All you're thinking at nine years of age is that it doesn't feel right. You may even attempt to set your mind at ease by saying to yourself this is a normal experience that most kids of your age go through. As you get older you realize this isn't the case. You know it wasn't right to be sexually attacked by your father, and as an adult, instead of feeling angry at the attacker you feel responsible for what has happened. Hence, feelings of fear, confusion and guilt shift into feelings of hurt, anger and premeditated violence. As an adult, it becomes difficult to rationalize the sexual abuse you've suffered by your father. Instead you may project the hurt and frustration onto an innocent target so you can feel some relief.

Let's continue with the abuse. As an adolescent you begin to resist the sexual advancements by your father, knowing that it isn't right. The important adult male figure in your life, whom you've loved and trusted, is now the target of anger, frustration, hatred and mistrust.

As you continue on the path of adolescence the pain you continue to suffer is repressed and rationalized as a normal occurrence. Even though rationalized, every detail of your life is affected. The abuse affects your psyche consciously and unconsciously as you adhere to your daily activities.

The serial killer deals with his anger, guilt and frustration by projecting his thoughts onto his victim. In the previous example, if your response to the sexual abuse is confusion, guilt and fear alone then you would be less likely to commit violence. If your emotions are consumed with hate, anger, frustration and rage, then you are likely to become a serious threat to the public. If all the above emotions are accelerated simultaneously then you are likely to slip into a psychotic state that manifests certain psychotic features. If this were the case it would progress itself over a lengthy period of time. Hence, the behavior that manifests itself according to the mental disorder is usually unpredictable: for example, sudden workplace violence. Many of the individuals who commit extreme workplace violence suffer from bipolar disorder or major depression, with some sort of psychotic episode. It's the period associated with mania when these people find enough energy to complete extreme acts of violence.

Chapter VIII

ORIGINS OF ANGER

Let's pretend you develop into a full-blown serial killer. Within the normal functioning range, if there's such a thing, beginning formations of anger predominate your psyche. In an attempt to maintain sanity, you project your anger onto the targeted victim rather than experience the emotional pain for yourself. In a sense your mind is protecting you from feeling depressed.

We all know that in an alarming state of depression people can have suicidal thoughts or suicidal ideation. Both sets of behavior are learned maladaptive traits. For example, you kill in order to keep your mind intact. Hence, you release your anger onto someone else. The anger released onto your victim is transformed into several sexual connotations, or fetishes, as we call them. For example, the intent of the attack is driven by anger itself. However, the anger is premeditated by a sexual component.

Before the murder is committed the perpetrator's angry feelings exist within his subconscious thought. Hence, the excitement phase or sexual component lies between the unconscious and subconscious layers of his psyche. When the attack occurs both the perpetrator's conscious feelings of anger and sexual frustration are released onto his victim. This brings us to the debate on serial killers either being sane or insane. That most serial killers are conscious and fully aware, when they select and abduct their victim, is food for thought. Murder itself may be subject to questioning and legal debate. However, most serial killers maintain jobs, drive a car, pay rent, and so on; of course there are exceptions to this general rule.

When you think of a practical serial killer think of Jekyll and Hyde. For example, serial killers are believed to have split personalities? Ted Bundy was a charming man with a friendly and inviting personality. Could you imagine what it must have been like to see his other side?

The thought pattern for Ted Bundy and other serial killers alike is effectively managing their anger in order to disguise their incipient criminal personality; thus, making their target unaware of their intentions to harm them. Ted Bundy's origin of anger was fueled just after he was dumped by the girlfriend he loved in college. Hence, the incident precipitated his pre-existing sadistic thought process that stemmed from early childhood. He murdered young beautiful girls who closely resembled the looks of his girlfriend and continued his path of rage for many years to follow.

Most of the adolescents I've spoken to break the law at an early age. Their behavior is modeled after an older individual, either a friend, a relative, or parent. Each crime the child gets away with is unconsciously being reinforced. Hence, the child will continue to break the law until he or she gets caught. The same goes for the serial killer or any other criminal who keeps getting away.

Most of the adolescents I've spoken to suffer from several learning disabilities and have usually had a parent who's been in trouble with the law. Learning disabilities are caused by a combination of genetics and predisposing factors of the child's surrounding environment. Not being able to read and write can cause a considerable amount of anger and frustration for an adolescent trying to discover his identity. To predict a child's potential for murder we must look at the way he or she filters his/her own anger and frustration. Second, we must look and see where he or she falls into the social spectrum. A good indicator would possibly be from a child who enjoys being all alone. Although there is no definitive answer to violence we must be aware of those we study in captivity. The most important indicator of violence is the child's thought process. There are many testing instruments to assess violent thought processes. However, they are rarely accurate. Many times a child or adolescent will verbally tell his friends or family what is going to happen. This is like a last-ditch effort to try and stop someone from committing acts of violence. Verbal warnings are a conscious cry for help. As we have seen in the case of such threats in public schools, they should not be taken lightly.

Throughout the 1990s increasing numbers of children committed acts of violence. I can't sit here and tell you the definitive causes of this increase. All I can say is, we don't have the answer to its decline.

I will serve as your guide as we enter into the realm of madness as most of the young murderers and rapists see it themselves. Hence, we will touch upon the commonalities that most of these adolescents share with each other.

Again, it's next to impossible to predict the future outcome of violence. The reason why it's so difficult to predict future violence is because most extremely violent men suffer from some type of organic brain damage which is usually invisible in behavioral terms. Hence, we are unable to predict the behavior patterns that attribute themselves to their pathology. However, if a serial killer doesn't suffer from a head injury or brain abnormality, his disposition is likely to be reinforced by genetics and the environment. Research studies have shown a genetic component that leads to violent behavior.

Research methods have proved that offspring of aggressive mothers or fathers tend to possess aggressive personality traits, even when raised apart. This can happen during the beginning stages of childhood. For instance, psychoanalytic theory upholds that an infant is born as a blank slate. The mother projects her own feelings onto the infant. Hence, these feelings usually consist of love, respect and a sense of dedication. In a few cases the mother projects the hate she has for herself onto her infant. Hence, this stage is where humans are most vulnerable. It is the time when we process information through modeling the behavior of significant others. In extreme cases a mother's intolerable hatred for herself is transformed onto the child. As a result, the child's psyche splinters off and forms the beginning stages of hatred. This section of the mind forms its own barriers and reacts violently, if challenged.

Chapter IX
MAN'S WORST ENEMY: IS HE THE DEVIL?

We've devoted much of our time to the serial killers who've been victims of physical, sexual and emotional abuse. What about the killers who have never suffered from any form of abuse at all? These guys are the likes of Ted Bundy. Actually, the Ted Bundys are the worst kinds of serial killers because their methodical state of mind and intense passion for killing are their primary motivating force. Also, they're very difficult to catch. These types of serial killers possess a sharp, witty mind and enjoy the thrill of the hunt and subsequent fatal attack. Their strength increases after each kill. Finally, they strike out of passion and have a insatiable appetite for watching the victim struggle. The victim's struggle facilitates the attacker's sexual fantasies of power and control. Many serial killers act out sexually on their victim post-mortem by masturbating at the scene of the crime, or at a later date. Usually the killer takes some of the victim's belongings. Law enforcement officials refer to these possessions as trophies. Hence, such trophies can be as meaningless to us as the victim's driver's license.

Again, many serial killers perform sexual acts on their victims post-mortem. In some cases for the serial killer sex is more comfortable after the victim dies for reasons of sexual inadequacies. Sexual inadequacies range from erectile dysfunctions to premature ejaculation. The reasons for these sexual limitations vary with each individual. However, most serial killers who commit sexual acts post-mortem act out their fantasy and reveal their fetishes without interruption.

Hence, they're embarrassed of their own sexual limitations to go public. For instance, many of the male serial killers are thought to have erectile difficulties. They believe it's the victim's fault, usually a female's. Hence, they make females their primary target in an effort to mask their own homosexual tendencies.

An experienced serial killer is addicted to the rush of killing much like a drug addict is addicted to the effects of a drug. The rush is associated with the reactions of the victim as the killer attacks and the sense of control established during the attack. All of these components play a necessary part in the killer's motivations. However, one of the commonalities between all three motives is the sexual connotation behind each. Each act of violence serves the perpetrator's fantasies on how he sees it. Hence, each attack is mediated by these fantasies and it is revealed at the crime scene.

Again, there's always a story being told at the scene of a crime: for example, how the body is arranged, whether there's semen around the body, or on the victim's clothing. We can tell a lot about the perpetrator from his choice of weapon, how the victim was killed, whether there was sexual activity pre- or post-mortem, and what was either taken or left at the scene of the crime.

Usually, serial killers and serial rapists are narcissists. Their own narcissism eventually leads to their capture. For example, they can be cocky and leave subtle clues behind for authorities to see. They repeat the crimes and continue to leave clues. Eventually, they become careless and return to their old murder sites to relive their fantasies. It's almost as if they want authorities to discover the victim. Did you ever play hide-and-seek? During the beginning stages of hide-and-seek either you or your partner hides. Hence, the goal of the game is to find your partner before your time expires. Hours may go by and you still can't find the person in hiding. Eventually your friend becomes bored with the game and he attempts to broaden the stakes (take a risk) in order to make the game more interesting.

This is exactly what happens with most serial killers. They eventually become bored with the game and wish to reveal a bit more of themselves to broaden the stakes. This behavior is risky and they seem to get sloppy by leaving subtle clues at the scene of the crime. Their conscious intention is not to get caught but to reveal bits of information about themselves to make it easier to get caught. Who knows why they do this. Perhaps for notoriety or to challenge law enforcement officials.

Like hide-and-seek, if murder becomes too easy their desire to kill decreases. The serial killer's need for risk associated with capture must be maintained in order to facilitate the fantasy. Hence, a sense of high risk is maintained by the clues left behind at the scene of the crime, and in the risk used in disposing the victim's body.

Without selectively hunting or stalking the victim the killer's purpose to kill remains stagnant. Serial killers tend to seek out a victim just as a hunter seeks out its prey. It has to be a game but the ultimate wish is control. Imagine the amount of control the killer has. To determine if another human being will live or die is the essence of his desire. Hence, he lives by establishing a perceived sense of total control. Some rapists have the power to establish it without violence and some must kill in order to have it. In some cases, I don't know if it's as much control over the victim as it is control over the outcome of their subsequent fantasies. The serial killer perceives control at the very sight of the hunt while serial rapists tend to perceive control during and after the attack.

Again, serial killers tend to establish control during the onset of their hunt. A serial killer is mostly an opportunist. Hence, he looks for visible weaknesses in his prey just as a lion looks for a weak antelope. If the attacker is a healthy male and the potential victim is appealing, vulnerable and crippled, he or she makes an enticing target for the perpetrator. Hence, there is no confrontational advice to give the victim because there are all types of serial killers and serial rapists with different motives.

In almost all of the cases I've read about, serial killers do not have personal connections with most of their victims. According to the FBI this makes them difficult to catch. The geographical region of the killings and disposal of the body will have significant importance in the efforts leading to apprehension.

Serial killers may have stalked their victims for days, weeks or months. However, in that timeframe was there dialogue between the killer and his victim? If there was dialogue did the killer initiate it to perhaps size up his prey? By sizing up his prey, I mean putting together the whole package that meets the serial killer's fantasy. If he or she does not meet the needs of the serial killer's fantasy, then he will select a different victim. Once again, most serial killers are opportunistic killers. Sometimes their fantasy can be ruined by simply observing the way their potential victim walks, talks and smiles. It can be ruined by watching the victim's facial gestures before and during the attack. Hence, this is why some sexually sadistic individuals want their victim to repeat what they say and act in a certain way conducive to their twisted fantasy. For example, I've seen arrest reports that state that the perpetrator wants the victim to repeat: "Tell me that you want me, bitch", "I'm better than your husband, aren't I", or "Play dead for me, bitch."

Why would a violent man kill a person he doesn't know as opposed to a person he knows? First, serial killers who kill people they know are not classified as serial killers because of the intense emotional reaction to the situation. For example, a previous date decides to humiliate you in front of your classmates in school. The same day your parents punish you for coming home late. Hence, the next day you get fired at work. All of the aforementioned negative events can lead to violent behavior, especially if the person is stressed, angry, frustrated, depressed and has a genetic predisposition for aggressive behavior or subsequent brain pathology.

The killer, who tends to kill people he's connected to in

some way, is known as a spree killer. Spree killers are different from serial killers in some important ways. One is that serial killers usually have a pattern to their madness. For example, they are likely to select victims in a similar age range, race, sex, and so on. Hence, their motive is different from that of a spree killer. The serial killer relies on risk assessment tied into his fantasy that invariably plays itself out in a sexual manner. For example, a spree killer such as Andrew Cunanan, who killed Gianni Versace in front of his house, had many different methods to his madness. Cunanan's alleged victims before Versace, included a former lover, a real estate mogul in Chicago and a cemetery worker killed only for his truck. As you can see there is no set pattern or methodology tied to Cunanan's killings. His motives seem to be an act of revenge rather than acting out his sexual fantasies. Second, serial killers tend to methodically plan their attack and "cool off" in between their cycles of killing. Spree killers tend to act out with a more passionate motive for destruction and revenge and they set themselves up at a quick pace. Third, spree killers tend to kill quickly and rather often as opposed to serial killers who tend to kill people as their pastime. Serial killers usually hold down some sort of job and their motive to kill is driven by sexual desire. The serial killer prides himself on his kill and becomes better at it with practice. Details of a typical serial killer's sexual fantasies reveal themselves through the aftermath of the kill and what he does with the body. Some of the methods both serial killers and spree killers use raise new questions on whether or not mankind can be explained in generalized terms of evil versus good.

It certainly raises questions as to whether or not serial killers can be classified as normal human beings. Experts offer a wide range of beliefs in arriving at an answer to this query. However, all this does is set the stage for legal debate. For example, the theory or theorist who has the best explanation for the case at hand holds the most weight in court.

Violence can be premeditated and is usually learned as a

result of negative situations that occur in our environment. For example, if you were to physically harm people directly or indirectly involved with your personal misfortunes, you're acting out an emotional response to situations that have previously occurred. Hence, this is an example of how a learning theorist views premeditated violence. Your negative situation can possibly lead to violence towards a victim you perceive as directly or indirectly responsible for the pain you feel. For example, look what happened to the reputation of the United States Post Office. A few postal workers lost control of their lives and saw their job as their direct source of pain and discomfort. In a desperate attempt to cauterize their emotional pain they killed some of their coworkers.

Every man, woman and beast has a certain tolerance for pain associated with violence that is determined by biological mechanisms. For example, neurotransmitter release, synaptic transmission, and action potentials result in the movement of muscles that can initiate a violent act. Hence, if the threshold of excitation is met the neuron will fire, causing an abrupt change in behavior, otherwise known as an action potential. Therefore, violence can be an uncontrollable, physiological response associated with one's absolute threshold. The strength of one's threshold has a lot to do with one's protective factors. The postal workers' violent rage wasn't directed at any one person just as much as it wasn't directed towards the job itself. Simply, their thresholds of excitation were breached when they got fired. A perceived lack of social support (protective factors) weakened their absolute threshold, thus making them unpredictable and predisposing them to react violently at a faster pace.

The distraught postal worker is not classified as a serial killer because he has targeted people he's been associated with in the past. Hence, his vacation plans are indeed permanent. The postal worker is only classified as a serial killer if he travels abroad and murders people at random.

What causes emotionally reactive killers (mass murderers)

to blow their brains out at the end is their intense feelings of guilt. Rather than cope with the intense feelings of guilt they decide to pull the gun on themselves. Who knows why they kill themselves. Some people say that they just want to take people with them and it's their way of finally being heard and listened to? The fact is that these people are extremely hurt, volatile and depressed. Their impulsive act of violence doesn't happen overnight. It's an evolution that occurs as each event in the person's life is magnified tenfold.

There's a difference between one who kills as an emotional reactive response compared to a premeditated response such as a serial killer. The difference is that a serial killer's insatiable appetite for the hunt reflects no guilt or remorse for the violence he commits and the mess he always leaves behind. Mass murderers usually reflect an all or nothing effort to be heard. Again, serial killers have a "cooling off" period that establishes itself with each victim they kill; also, the serial killer tends to take his time with his approach as opposed to a mass murderer, who becomes engulfed by feverish emotion. The serial killer is usually guided by fantasy, while the mass murderer is usually guided by rage.

We have briefly touched on how a serial killer's fantasy possibly conflicts with reality and also on some of the major differences between mass murderers, spree murderers, and serial killers.

In the following paragraphs I will discuss a few important concepts of serial killers and how they displace reality: firstly, the likely signs of a serial killer and serial rapist; secondly, why serial killers kill people they do not know; and thirdly, when is the predisposition to kill at the highest point in the developmental cycle leading to violence? This brief synopsis is derived directly from case studies, books, journal articles, FBI reports and other research methodology.

Emotional incest is an invisible psychological component of sexual abuse that exists in the relationship between a parent and child. You'll see how the effects can possibly drive a person to commit violence.

A child who experiences emotional incest will likely be involved in an unstable relationship at least once in his life. Hence, it's usually the male in the relationship who has the predisposition to become violent.

Violence can occur when the male child in the family establishes himself as the protector of his mother. The behavior relative to this role facilitates the child's early sexual fantasies towards her. Hence, the child's mother leaves her son fixated at this stage of development by forming a protective barrier that enables her son to assume this role. The protective barrier is formed by mom's feelings of inadequacy towards herself. Hence, her negative feelings are projected onto her son. The protective barrier remains as a shield against feelings of guilt. This type of mother–son bond subsequently arrests the child's sexual and emotional progress. For instance, many theorists indicate that pedophiles are arrested or fixated at earlier stages of sexual development. Hence, their sexual prowess is consistent with their mental age.

Guilt is usually the end result of a child suffering from emotional incest. Hence, its effects can be noted in childhood, adolescence and early adulthood. In relationships he or she seeks an intimate partner who resembles his mother. However, he can develop a sadistic routine based on the guilt he feels. Hence, this occurs when he or she masks the direct opposite of how they're supposed to behave. For example, a boy who's been a victim of emotional incest is essentially forced into this role of caring and responsibility. Hence, he perceives himself as a dependence source and an emotional crutch. At the other end of the spectrum the boy fulfills a pre-oedipal wish of becoming the hero in his family.

The child's fantasies may backfire as he gets older. For example, in some cases the child's ego forces him to rebel against the personality trait that was bestowed upon him as a direct result of emotional incest. Hence, in this case the child would be less anxious by behaving directly opposite to who and what a hero is perceived to be.

A child perceives his mother's love as a necessity towards emotional growth and survival. The child is usually aware that he manifests sexual thoughts of intimacy towards his mother. In extreme cases of emotional incest usually the mother subconsciously wishes to be intimate with her son. Her need is facilitated emotionally rather than physically. However, the child usually picks up on it. Most of the time the child casts his mother's dependent personality aside, but hatred, anger and guilt may consume the child's psyche due to the reciprocal fantasies of lust towards each other. As a result, the child feels guilt towards his feelings of passion for his mother. Guilt is less violent than hate. However, guilt can form into hate and hate can be projected onto others in the form of violence. As for the child, anger and frustration are routed into acceptable forms of activity instead of physical violence. He still wishes to be intimate with his mother and relationships with the opposite sex will closely resemble the footsteps of his mother.

Chapter X

SERIAL KILLER PROFILES ON EMOTIONAL INCEST

The danger of emotional incest for sexual predators is when the young adult is rejected or hurt by women inside or outside the relationship, coupled by a perceived rejection by his mother.

These types of sexual predators primarily target female victims. The reason why they attack women is to initiate revenge on their own feelings of guilt. The revenge is sexual in nature because it's tied into Freud's Oedipal stage of eroticism and the wish to be with his mother. This involves incestuous demands to the son onto his mother. Anger is created at a subconscious level with the feeling that the young man will never get the opportunity to love his mother in the way his unconscious demands. The child's anger is a result of feeling guilt and a sense of inadequacy from not meeting his mother's sexual or physical standards.

The reason why forming a relationship with his mother in the future becomes so important to the child as a victim of emotional incest is a result of the role he assumed as a child. That is, protector, spouse, hero and caretaker. He fulfilled all these roles respectively, yet he still feels inadequate. The child feels he is still unable to conquer his mother's barriers to love him sexually. The term sexually is not limited to just the physical act, but to the broad spectrum of love, trust, truth and understanding.

Chapter XI
INTO THE REALMS OF FANTASY

Fantasy is an unconscious process of combining and transforming both internal and external inside the connections of reality. Sigmund Freud treated fantasy as an ego function and as a derivative of primary unconscious wishes. The unconscious wish becomes repressed and is later identified through dreams. The true nature of the serial killer's functional processes lay within the core of his dreams and fantasies.

The serial rapist's fantasies are brought to reality by the way he treats the victim during the actual rape itself. There are rapes aiming more at power reassurance or anger excitation. The anger rapist will inflict more pain on the victim, while the power rapist wishes to establish control with less violent means. The power rapist uses the victim to perhaps establish his sense of manhood. This rapist will sometimes apologize to the victim or give the victim some leeway. The anger rapist will sometimes kill the victim in order to gain control. Most of these perpetrators have an intense hatred towards women.

Dreams are formed in the systems of preconscious or conscious states. With that being said, the serial killer or serial rapist is able to identify with the representation of the dream wish. The dream wish is sexual in nature: meaning, the energy from the dream and its symbolic meaning are guided by internal sexual processes and the fulfillment of the dream wish is being acted out by killing and raping people.

Sexuality and fantasy are expressions of reality only to exist within the realm of impulse.

Unlike most of us, the serial killer acts out his dreams,

which, in turn, become his fantasies. The latent meaning of the dream is expressed through sources within the perpetrator's environment. These sources are the symbolic representations of the dream itself. The sources include, but are not limited to, victimology: for example, the perpetrator's personal preference for a particular personality type, sex, age, race, color, type of clothing and income. Some of these factors underline the motivational qualities of the serial killer's choice of victim.

Satisfaction from the killer's fantasy is obtained through an illusion he created. The killer separates himself from reality and the external world to become something other than himself. His other self is played out through the existing fantasy.

The fantasy is created through the ups and downs of the killer in relation to his or her own experiences. This is not an inherited fantasy where the person is born to think in this way. Instead, a complicated route is taken where the subject takes into account the objects presented to them throughout their lifespan and creates a scenario in which the unconscious effects come into play.

When the serial killer fantasizes about his potential victim, the eroticism of power and control facilitates the belief he can alter the situation of the victim. By imagining this he removes himself from a position in which he can suffer, alternatively in which he can inflict harm on someone else. Ultimately the death of the victim can be unconsciously perceived as, now, the victim is safe from me (the killer).

The attempts of the serial killer to perform his ritualistic patterns of murder coincide with an attempt to master his own personal conflicts.

Part of the serial killer's psychopathy stems from the difficulties of life's transitions coupled with a lack of protective factors.

To touch again on protective factors: they are barriers that keep a mind sane. These include, love, companionship, strong family guidance and support, educational background, employment status, and so on.

Most serial killers are young to middle-aged white males who have difficulties making normal life transitions, coupled with the sexual, physical, or emotional abuse they've most likely suffered as a child. A weakness in protective factors and mid-life transitions can lend a hand to violent acts.

The fantasy mingles with reality and causes aggressive acts in relation to frustration, loss and pain. The fantasy dictates the perpetrator to be within psychic reach of the victim before his initial confrontation. Only then can the threshold of the fantasy take place within his psychic bounds. For example, the killer must wish to dominate, abuse, humiliate, and make the victim suffer as he continues to suffer. In this case, the motive of the fantasy is revenge: revenge for what goddamn person has made he or she become; or, is it revenge for what happened to the killer in the past? These questions, along with others can be revealed in the serial killer's dreams and fantasies.

Chapter XII

BRAIN INJURY AND PSYCHOPATHY

In the United States, approximately two to three per cent of all rapes end up in violence. Less than two per cent end up in murder, while less than one per cent of violent crimes involve serial murder. These statistics may not be eye-popping to traditional American culture; however, serial murder, serial rape, and other violent crimes manage to maintain a steady level throughout the years, without a substantial increase or decline. Acts of extreme violence are indeed rare, but are becoming more popular as we step into the new millennium.

Research during the early and mid 1990s has shown that people who suffer from brain injuries such as cerebral contusions or moderate/severe concussions have signs of aggressive and impulsive behavior patterns accompanied with a complicated and long-term recovery process.

What does this statement do for the purposes of this chapter? Well, we already know from previous research on serial killers, provided almost exclusively by the FBI's Behavioral Assessment Unit in Quantico, Virginia, that most violent predators suffered from some type of physical, and/or sexual abuse by parents or significant others. During the time these individuals suffered from physical and sexual abuse I wonder how many times the violence ended with multiple closed head injuries.

In a closed head injury there has been no actual penetration of brain tissue and the trauma is confined to cortical or subcortical regions of the brain. Once we suffer brain damage the cells cannot repair themselves. In other words, the damage is permanent. An example of a closed head injury during an abusive encounter would be person A striking person B in the head with a blunt object.

The brain damage suffered may go undiagnosed for years. You will see no observable damage to the structure of the brain. Everything will look and feel like it's intact. However, what you will not notice are the subtle and un-diagnosable changes in the brain cells such as the neurons, which manipulate behavior. Being struck on the head numerous times may damage not only neuronal functioning, but it can permanently damage blood vessels in the brain that may interfere with nutrient and oxygen supply to different brain areas that regulate normal physical and mental functioning. Some of the regions of the brain associated with impulse control, could be affected by the damage. For example, one case referred to me involved an inmate who had been struck on the front of the head by a brick during a fight. Most of the inmates who knew him said that, following the incident, his personality changed overnight. As a matter of fact, one of his friends warned a correction officer that something bad might happen. As a matter of fact, it did. The inmate I speak of was in the cafeteria lunch line and he thought someone cut him in line. He ran up to the man whom he thought had cut him in line and struck him in the head with a tray. Subsequent MRI and brain pathology reports found increased levels of vasopressin and decreased levels of serotonin in the subcortical regions of his brain.

Again, research has made a strong case for a causal relationship between brain injury and violence. Research in the late 1970s and early 80s has shown that a number of accidental injuries, brain pathology and violent victimization have occurred more frequently with juvenile delinquents with violent arrest histories than with non-juvenile delinquents.

Lewis, Pincus, Feldman, Jackson and Bard (1986) conducted an experiment on fifteen inmates who were facing the death penalty. All fifteen inmates had some history of head injuries with both major or minor neurological impairment.

Also, almost half the inmates had psychological illness accompanying neurological impairment.

In a subsequent study, Lewis, Pincus, Bard, Richardson, Prichep, Feldman and Yeager performed a battery of psychiatric, neuropsychological, educational and neurological evaluations on a group of juvenile murderers sentenced to death for the crime of murder. Approximately twenty-five per cent were found to have major neurological impairments, approximately twenty per cent had psychotic disorders predating their incarceration, another twenty per cent showed significant signs of organic impairment and only tow of the juvenile inmates had full IQ scores above ninety, which is still considered to be below normal. Twelve juveniles out of the thirty-seven sampled during the study had been sodomized by relatives.

Research provides relevance into some of the issues of mitigation and competency. Of course, we would need to look into the validity of the testing procedures, i.e. look at all the components to the nature, attitude and testing environment of the subjects being tested.

What could this reveal about serial killers? Are they insane because of brain damage? Or are they just plain old insane? I will shed one very crucial, important point on the subject of insanity and that is the nature of intent to commit the crime. One thing about serial killers that separates their crimes from the rest is the nature of their intent to commit violence.

Serial killers behave just like you and me, except that they possess "polar opposites" to their personalities. In Jungian terms, instead of their dark personality being repressed as the shadow it reveals itself as a selective part of the individual's persona, or how he views himself in the world.

A serial killer's intent focuses around the ability to know right from wrong. If he didn't know right from wrong then he wouldn't be able to function with daily activities or blend in with the rest of society. For example, the thought process is like this: it's right to work because I need money. It's wrong to kill and I know it, that's why I'm avoiding authorities.

Most serial killers are able to function with normal daily life activities and they know it's wrong to kill because they consciously avoid being captured. Furthermore, they're able to effectively communicate with others, hold down jobs, and take care of themselves in relatively good fashion.

The serial killers who have suffered severe physical and sexual abuse or head trauma usually learn to effectively cope with their physiological and psychological limitations. One of the ways in dealing with these limitations is actually going out and killing people in an effort to temporarily alleviate their pain and suffering in the world they were brought into, or as perceive themselves, a victim of. As adults, most serial killers are completely irredeemable. However, there are a few exceptions if they are given treatment in prison. How often does this occur? Prison usually doesn't treat behavior. It manages behavior. Prison is not a culpable force for their rehabilitation. They will have to make the choice to rehabilitate themselves. Most of the men convicted of multiple homicide, not already on death row, will never see the light of day in which their rehabilitation will be put to use for the benefit of society. Although some people will argue that most, if not all these men deserve to live the rest of their lives behind bars.

Chapter XIII
THE NATURE OF THE AGGRESSOR

There does seem to be a small percentage of the population characterized by recurrent violence and other antisocial behavior since childhood and early adolescence. In recent research literature on psychopathy and antisocial personality disorder (two of the more common behavioral traits of serial murderers) only three per cent of the male and female population exhibits or is diagnosed with the behavioral traits of these disorders. Subsequent studies related to this topic identified that psychopaths in the criminal system are responsible for most of the crime, and their offenses are more violent and aggressive in nature compared to the rest of men in the criminal system. Not all violent sociopaths are psychotic and not all psychotics are sociopaths. One common element between most sociopaths is their long history of arrests. They are otherwise known as repeat or chronic offenders. Laurence Miller found in chronic offender delinquents, six per cent were responsible for seventy-one per cent of the homicides, seventy-three per cent of the rapes, and sixty-nine per cent of the aggravated assaults (Tracy, Wolfgang and Figlio, 1990). Many of the apprehended serial killers have histories of prior arrests or institutionalization. However, they're not necessarily chronic offenders.

In the case of serial killers and sadistic rapists psychopathic aggression is often cold, callous, and methodical, but psychopaths are also liable to outbursts of impulsive rage and aggression. Is this to say that serial killers and sadistic rapists are not liable to spontaneous outbursts of impulsive rage? Not only are serial killers and sadistic rapists liable to spontaneous outbursts of impulsive rage but they can become more violent and establish greater control of their impulsiveness, even as their rage and aggression exacerbate into violence. For example, usually serial killers are poised in their attack as if it were a job. Fits of rage are more conducive to unexpected circumstances other than their work of stalking, killing or raping their victims. The other side of their personality allows them to assume a different role when luring their victims in for the kill.

Research on brain injury and violent crime, has yielded to a general clinical personality profile, which may or may not be conducive to every serial killer or serial rapist. This includes a hidden mask of superficial charm concealing their inner fantasies of self-worth, and a need for constant excitement and stimulation of the senses. Part of the serial killer's thrill in searching for vulnerable victims is the massive amounts of driving, indicated in research reports. Also, there seems to be a certain degree of increased levels of impulsivity. Hence, this can be evident through the killer's polar opposites of personality, or better referred to as the "Jekyll and Hyde" theory of personality previously mentioned. Both serial killers and anger rapists possess low reflectivity, poor self-control, shallow affect, lack of empathy, lack of remorse, manipulative behavior, a parasitic and exploitive lifestyle, social and moral irresponsibility and have difficulty in sustaining intimate relationships. Put all this together and you have a potentially dangerous individual.

You cannot compare a serial sadistic rapist to a serial killer because of two important reasons. These reasons reflect their different motives for the crime and methods of operation. However, they can be similar in respect to fulfilling the perpetrator's wish or fantasy that is mostly sexual in nature.

The rapist's motive usually centers around power reassurance and control. The serial killer's motive can range from either revenge, fulfilling a sexual desire, and deriving national attention often associated with serial killers. If any of these is the case then the act of killing brings the serial killer's fantasies to life. He will kill time and again to relive his fantasy. Hence, if the act itself didn't fulfill the killer's fantasy he will be unsatisfied; thus, he will kill again until he is.

Unfortunately, serial killers are rarely satisfied. They are often somewhat a bit dissatisfied with each kill because one thing usually goes wrong during the time of the attack or abduction. This is why most crime scenes of serial killers show post-mortem activity on their victim. Hence, the killer is comfortable in killing the victim to relive his fantasy which usually identifies itself sexually.

Most rapists and serial killers alike keep their victims alive because their fantasies are being met during the attack. Even before the attack the rapist's fantasy becomes a part of reality. In those weening seconds before the attack the rapist knows he's in control of that person's life. Remember, the perception of control is important for serial rapists in the same way as it applies with serial killers.

murder, before or after, can fulfill an inner sexual desire, this doesn't mean it has to be pornographic in nature. Many serial killers derive their fantasies from the context of their own psyche as they see themselves in relation to their victim. Serial killers can be inspired to kill when pornography is paired with violence.

6. "All serial killers have had poor childhood upbringing."
Research shows that most serial killers have suffered from some type of abuse. However, most of these accounts are not factual because the information is from the perpetrator himself. Unless they were hospitalized or HRS was involved from the alleged abuse there would be no record of the abuse ever happening. Serial killers such as Ted Bundy came from an average family background.

How does a man like Ted Bundy fall into the path of violence? Unfortunately, there is no one answer to this complicated question because nobody knows where the string snaps. An unexplained phenomenon over time catapults a man's psyche into violent thoughts. His violent thought process eats away at himself until he dies inside. When the killer is psychically dead it's easier for him to kill another. Hence, he'll go on ruthless killing sprees with cooling-off periods in order to fulfill trivial sexual fantasies. His motivation to kill can go on for years until he's eventually captured. The phenomenon that sets them off is never just one thing. It's a developmental process of many things that can be compacted into one thing that sets the killer off into his pattern of homicide. The question is where does the final string break?

7. "You are able to pinpoint a serial killer ahead of time."
The fact that they cannot be identified in advance is what places serial killers in their own elite body of offenders that makes them difficult to catch. They have no prior physical or emotional attachment to the victim, and they kill outside of money and greed. They're only identifiable by the destructiveness they leave behind. The FBI's elite

Behavioral Science Unit attempts to find the personality of the offender by looking at the method and manner in which the crime was carried out. A fancy name for this method is "criminal investigative analysis".

8. "All serial killers possess sexually violent tendencies."
Some serial killers possess sexually sadistic fantasies and thought patterns. However, many of them are not sexual sadists. A diagnosis for sexual sadism implies that the "fantasies, sexual urges, or behaviors cause clinically significant distress or impairment in social, occupational, or other important areas of functioning." (DSM-IV 245) Remember, most serial killers are effectively able to maintain employment status. Serial rapists, particularly anger rapists, are more likely to fit these diagnostic criteria.

9. "Serial killer's choice of victim resembles a family member, mainly a parental figure."
Obviously, this is not always the case. You may have heard this a few times in literature in the context of psychoanalytic babble. In reality, this may be the case only for a few serial killers, but certainly not all. Psychoanalysis carries the notion that males during childhood (phallic stage) possess sexual and/or erotic fantasies of pursuing their mother sexually. Their wish is to destroy their father and to live with the mother happily ever after. With women it's vice versa. A healthy functioning individual will grow out of these thoughts quickly and establish healthy relationships with the opposite sex. However, trouble can occur if the mother takes it upon herself and brings her son's fantasies to life, either physically or emotionally during this crucial stage of development. We will be able to tell how the child reacts by the way his mother detaches herself from the incestuous relationship with her son. An important point to know is that physical incest is more common in father/daughter relationships, and emotional incest is more common in mother/son relationships. Both can have adverse effects on the victim as he or she enters

into the different phases of human development.

10. "Serial killers wish to be captured by the authorities."

    They don't want to get caught as much as they want the bodies of their victims to be discovered. Serial killers derive satisfaction within themselves for what they accomplish in their killings. They want everyone else to see what they've accomplished and got away with. This is one of the reasons why they'll steal trophies and little reminders of the victim and the event that previously took place. They also enjoy making law enforcement officers look incompetent. Sometimes they'll hang out in police bars and overhear details in their case. When they're captured they want to know how they compare with everyone else.

11. "Serial killers have absolutely no morals."

    Generally this has been found to be true with almost all serial killers. However, I am willing to challenge research findings and ask my readers what morality really is. It is the principle of what an individual perceives as being right or wrong. One individual may believe it is morally wrong to lie or cheat, yet most people have lied before. One murderer I spoke with in prison mentioned that he helped an old lady with her groceries because she was having a hard time in the ice and snow. He must have watched seven people go by and nobody assisted the old lady with her groceries. One could argue that this convicted murderer considered it immoral not to help the old lady. What if serial killers had their own specific moralistic code such as the previous example? On the opposite end of the spectrum of lying and cheating, killing total strangers at random is generally considered immoral but morality is defined in terms of individuality and subjectivity. That is the very principle for which it exists.

It's difficult to pinpoint a serial killer's exact motive because of the diversity of the human psyche. It's like trying to predict the weather. For example, when we see overcast skies we usually expect rain. However, sometimes a cold front moves in and most of the clouds disappear. The same theory applies in predicting the behavior of serial killers. Many serial killers possess universal characteristics such as fire-setting, late bed-wetting, animal cruelty and antisocial personality traits. However, there's always one important characteristic that is unique for each serial killer. When this unique characteristic is revealed it makes them much easier to catch. We must remember that human behavior isn't an exact science.

Chapter XV
MORTAL SIN

It's interesting to reflect on your past and see how you've ended up where you are, at this very moment. One day I found myself working as a head tennis coach and then I found myself behind the steel doors of a federal prison. I've encountered men who have done some of the most awful things to others. Yet, I constantly fought within myself because I could see nothing wrong with these men.

I recall one inmate whom I could easily see myself spending time with on the street. He was a likeable fellow and around the same age as me. I didn't want to look at his charges because I knew it would negatively influence the therapeutic process. After several lengthy sessions I eagerly wanted to know what he did to put himself in prison. When he told me he was sentenced in prison for life I immediately knew it was murder. He glared straight into my eyes and told me that I knew what he did. I will tell his story as he told it to me.

> I saw her standing across the counter in the pub–restaurant and bar. Her light-brown shorts revealed the crease of the pattern of her underwear. Goddamn, she has a nice ass. I wonder if she's wearing a G-string or regular underwear? It looks like regular underwear to me. I just want to rip into her flesh and bite her neck as hard as I can.

> Her verbal and facial reaction is the first step in fulfilling my fantasy and it will make me feel good in the process. How she responds to me will determine whether or not I rape her or kill her. If I say "Hi" she needs to respond the way I want her to. If she does not it will make me more angry. I want to hear her scream when I tear off her clothes and force her knees to

touch her face. I think she'll scream pretty good. I can tell because of her lips.

My thoughts are not only about death but sexual desire. I want to hear her scream and see the blood pour from her neck and mouth. I want to bite her legs and watch her squirm. The intention is not for her to be killed but to feel the pain I initiate. You know it's my pain she feels. Only when she stops squirming I will know what peace feels like for a while.

The only reason why I might not decide to rape this beautiful waitress is the moral implications tied to the act itself. Also, I can face jail time, or if she dies, possibly face the death penalty. What if I get caught?

These factors significantly deter most potential serial killers and rapists from committing serious crimes. However, it did not deter this inmate I spoke with.

For the serial killers who decide to commit murder, morality does not exist for at least a while. Instead, they are concerned with the release of hostility and hate towards the world and their victim. The hate is manifested through intense sexual desire, which is targeted on their potential victim. The inmate I spoke with had a genuine hatred towards women because he'd always been rejected by them.

Setting the inmate aside, I really believe there's some sort of a mechanism in the brain that keeps potential serial killers from committing heinous acts on other human beings. The killer I interviewed cared nothing for the rights of the waitress he murdered. He quotes, "To me she's nothing but a piece of meat." It's the aftermath of the event that concerns the killer. They just don't want to go to prison. If serial killers can find an acceptable outlet for their fantasies then killing wouldn't be a part of their repertoire. Usually, the outlet exists in some form of masturbation. Masturbating towards their victim may occur immediately post-mortem, or it may exist days, months or years after they have killed their victims. If masturbation occurs at the sight of the murder then we're looking at what the FBI's Behavioral Resource Unit refers to as the disorganized perpetrator. Also, he would tend to be more impulsive.

One that masturbates at his own residence usually keeps personal items of the people he kills. He tends to be more of what the FBI refers to as an organized perpetrator. He is likely to be less risky or impulsive than the disorganized perpetrator, but after a few murders he may get bold and attack during the day hours and choose a more difficult victim. For example, a successful child serial killer may decide to attack a more challenging victim, such as a handicapped adult. Hence, organized perpetrators are much more difficult to catch than disorganized ones. Many disorganized perpetrators will have prior psychiatric hospitalizations, or have a pre-existing criminal history.

Now back to the inmate I interviewed. He was able to rationalize his thought processes by effectively thinking about his fantasy in a relaxed state of mind. The more angry at women he became, the more he thought about ripping his victim's (waitress) flesh. The more angry he became the less inhibitions he had at the time he killed this young woman. Hence, his lack of control is partly due to the amounts of testosterone that were released by his neurotransmitters during the time of the attack. The physiological event took place as follows: as the inmate's neurons fired they released testosterone throughout his entire body. Hence, it caused him to think, feel and behave aggressively. What initially keeps the transmitter substances in check is the relative control we have in our lives. Just before the inmate killed the waitress he lost his job, his father died, and his mother kicked him out of the house because he was using drugs. The less control we perceive in our lives the less control our physiological instincts have.

I interviewed a convicted child pornographer in prison and this is what he told me. "The closest I came to killing a girl was at a movie theatre. She was with her boyfriend and she had the best body I'd ever seen. She didn't even look at me. I thought of ways to get her away from her boyfriend so I could kidnap and rape her. What stopped me from committing this crime was the thought of going to prison, and that's all." You see there are many people like the inmate I interviewed who've had violent thoughts such as these. This convicted child pornographer is a far cry from a serial killer. However, their motivation for their crime tends to be sexual in nature.

What separates this convicted child pornographer from a serial killer, besides financial gain? The individuals who have managed to control a lust for murder haven't reached their absolute threshold of anger and frustration. Hence, many of their protective factors remain intact. For instance, they maintain their sanity by having a good paying job, a stable family and good health. Serial killers have reached their threshold and acted on its behalf because of limited protective factors in their lives. Their thresholds possess so much hate for the world. Hence, their intolerable hatred for the world consumes their thoughts and allows them to commit murder after murder without remorse, because of the hate connected to their crime.

Their anger becomes controlled by the split personalities they possess. This is one of the major reasons why they become successful predators. This occurs because their personalities are the extreme opposite of each other when they stalk their potential victims. For instance, think of Ted Bundy, the professor who murdered the college coeds. He was successful in establishing a friendly and charming personality. You would never imagine this man had consumed so much hate. Possibly, Ted Bundy derived sexual pleasure by seeing the look of shock in the victim's eyes just before he violently attacked them. For the victim to see this charming man, with the flip of a hat, turn into a monster must have been a sexually stimulating experience for Bundy. Initially, as soon as he had control over the fate of his victim his personality changed from being a charming man to becoming an angry killer. Bundy didn't kill his victims while they were unconscious. He wanted them to see his other personality. Both personalities are employed within Ted Bundy's as well as any other serial killer's psyche in order to create a more efficient predator.

This is one of the reasons why serial killers like Ted Bundy become better at what they do. They are effectively able to work with, and overcome, their weaknesses of both personalities. As a result, they become more comfortable when they eventually lure their victims into their often-fatal trap.

Chapter XVI
PEDOPHILES IN PRISON

When we think of prison we think of people being locked in cages for a very long time. We label a man or a woman as bad if they've served time in prison. But what about the change aspect, or what the criminal justice system refers to as rehabilitation? Can prisoners change? Yes, they can. However, it's probably the most difficult for sexual offenders to change, especially pedophiles.

What is a pedophile? A pedophile is diagnosed in the category of DSM-IV as a "sexual paraphilia" or sexual disorder that involves sexual activity with a prepubescent child (generally thirteen years or younger). The individual with pedophilia must be at least sixteen years of age or older and at least five years older than the child. For individuals in adolescence diagnosis must rely on good clinical judgment. (DSM-IV, 1994)

I've interviewed grown men in prison (age forty-three or older) involved in child pornography rings or having sexual relations with eleven- and twelve-year-old boys and girls. One particular inmate I interviewed informed me that he had sold over two thousand pornographic magazines and videotapes to the public. Ultimately, if it ever got out in the general population of the prison that this inmate's charge was child pornography he would be in grave danger. For some reason inmates do not like this breed of criminal. If the opportunity presented itself the other inmates would attack a child pornographer, pedophile, rapist and serial murderer. Perhaps they do it for attention, or it's an easy way to make a name for themselves by killing a famous serial killer, or a child pornographer.

Why is it that treating pedophiles or any other type of sexual offender is very difficult, if not impossible? For one thing, we have to look at their sexual prowess as an addiction. Hence, they're addicted to having sex, fantasizing about sex and manipulating young children because they're easy to control. Hence, in the perpetrator's case he's facilitating a sexual fantasy based on the feeling that children provide a sense of lost innocence in his life. Hence, by establishing a relationship with a young child he's recapturing the innocence and failures of loss that occurred at one point in his life.

Currently, laws are becoming much stiffer for some of these individuals to be released from prison. For example, the Florida State Legislature has initiated the Jimmy Ryce Act. Basically, this Act implies that most sexual offenders are not fit to be released into society. Hence, this law makes it very difficult for sexual offenders and pedophiles to be released from prison after their term is up. In order to be released they must be evaluated immediately when their prison term is up by a licensed psychiatrist or psychologist specializing in this area. The Act stipulates that if the licensed psychologist or psychiatrist determines that they are unfit for society they're to be recommitted to prison.

Even though the Jimmy Ryce Act infringes on the constitutional rights of individuals it will probably protect innocent victims in the future, especially if the perpetrator doesn't receive any treatment during his prison term. If aversion and cognitive and hormonal therapies are offered as treatment modalities within the prison system then they'll stand a much better chance in being rehabilitated when their prison term expires. However, offering such programs in prison is dangerous for the perpetrators themselves. For example, the word may get out to the other inmates that inmate X is a sexual offender or pedophile. To increase the safety of these inmates, perhaps prison systems can set up separate placement wards for sexual offenders, giving them restricted access to the general prison population and vice versa.

Why are children at risk when pedophiles are released from prison without treatment? The first thing a prisoner will say near the end of his prison term is, "I've changed since I've been in prison." Of course, they've changed. Their environment is restricted enough to where it's difficult for them to act out. I refer to this type of change as "temporary compliance". For an incarcerated sexual offender, the mere fact there are no women and children to victimize, plays into this concept of change. Another factor is that the individual will have to face a lot more stressors on the outside than the inside. Hence, a free individual has total freedom to make his own choices. Moreover, temporary compliance involves temporary change in his behavior with little or no change in his cognitive thought processes.

Behavioral tasks are easy to alter, especially if they're enforced in a strict environment such as a prison. Cognitive or mental change takes a considerable amount of time for a pedophile to alter. Only with long-term treatment focused on the disorder itself and its symptomatology will change progress.

The most important aspect of change is from the individual him/herself. He has to have a strong willingness and desire to change if any treatment modality is to work. Additionally, he has to accept the fact that he has a problem. Many sex offenders and pedophiles I've interviewed in prison believe they're not only innocent but that they've done nothing wrong. One of the most popular statements I've heard from pedophiles is, "She wanted me to love her."

Many factors can affect the treatment of pedophiles. Pedophiles must accept it within themselves that there is a problem. Quite frankly, I've found many of them do not meet this very important criterion. Second, they must have the willingness to make the necessary steps for change. If they're in denial, how are they going to make these changes? The fact of the matter is they won't. They may not necessarily re-offend, but their mental process is not altered.

If the court decides to release a pedophile from prison without treatment, think of this scenario. You drive past a sign on the corner of a gas station that reads DANGER in big red words. You get out of the car to find that underneath the sign lies a leaky gas pump. Ten years later you pass that same gas station and the DANGER sign is still there. It will always remain standing if no one bothers the leaky gas pump. However, if one day I decide to strike a match under it, it will possibly explode.

The point is, if you release a pedophile from prison and he/she encounters a young child, then it's likely you'll see the same behavior (explosion) that put him/her in prison. Also, he may re-offend on a more escalated level. For example, he may kill his victim this time because he's afraid of getting caught and being sent back to prison.

This is possible because each offence is based on a developmental continuum. For example, the pedophile may not have started out as a pedophile. He may have been previously arrested for voyeurism (peeping tom) or exhibitionist behavior (exposing your body parts to the public). The victim's reaction to an exhibitionist's acts seems to reinforce his behavior. Voyeuristic behavior is likely to occur after exhibitionistic behavior occurs because voyeurism appears to be more serious. Hence, voyeurism could possibly be a stepping-stone for other serious crimes such as burglary and even rape.

Again, exhibitionism, voyeurism and rape can lead to advanced criminal activity. For example, whatever the case may be a pedophile, rapist, or any other sexual offender may become bold in regard to his methodology and initiate contact with his victim. Hence, their sole purpose is to relive the ultimate fantasy, whatever it may be to them in a subjective sense of the term. Unfortunately, these fantasies rarely get played out to perfection. As a result, many sexual perpetrators are unsatisfied. Hence, they continue to seek the perfect victim. When they don't find him/her they just get more frustrated.

A pedophile can become violent if he comes to the realization that he cannot control and maintain his relationship with the prepubescent child. Hence, he may be more abrupt in dealing with this realization by raping and sometimes murdering the child. Some may curtail their approach in accidentally killing a child in order to initiate and maximize their fantasies and sometimes they'll kill the child for fear of being discovered.

Chapter XVII
STALKING

A woman working as a bartender at San Antonio airport told me a brief story about a friend of hers who was being followed by a stranger. The bartender's story inspired me to write this chapter. She explained that her friend was very attractive and she had a bad habit of attracting strange men. This particular man had flowers delivered to her once a week whether she was at home or work. Not once had he left his name; hence, the card always read blank inside.

This man can be referred to as a secret admirer. Hence, it has a more positive connotation than the term "stalker". I mentioned to the bartender that this secret admirer doesn't have to be a man. Plenty of women wish to make themselves anonymous when they are attracted to the same sex, especially if they don't know the other person's sexual preference. However, after hearing more about the young woman, I assumed it was a man who was following her and sending her flowers.

Let's say the woman's secret admirer is a man. Because he sends her flowers he most likely has harmless intentions except a wish to be close to the girl. Why? Because flowers represent growth and beauty. In sending flowers this person is revealing his wish to grow with this young woman in a relationship of some sort. The red roses themselves can represent growth, beauty and romance. For example, any rose or flower takes time to bloom. The gift represents the stalker's wish to be near the person he admires in time. The flowers also serve as a symbolic representation of the secret admirer himself. For example, he's delivering a part of himself to the girl as roses because he's not ready to reveal himself in human form.

The idea of giving represents wanting to share with another person. Sharing is a major component of building and sustaining a healthy relationship. So at some point this particular secret admirer has had fantasies of forming a relationship with this young woman. Sharing can also be the prerequisite for caring.

I venture an educated guess based on the only evidence presented that this man is merely a secret admirer and he doesn't mean the bartender's friend any serious harm. In extreme cases of secret admiration the secret admirer will look out for the admired one. The danger occurs when the stalker will not stop following you until he gets what he wants out of his victim. In this story I was talking about instances of a somewhat normal individual. Haven't you ever sent flowers to someone secretly?

What separates a secret admirer from a stalker? Or do they go hand in hand with each other? A secret admirer admires the person for who they are or what he/she perceives them to be. It can be their external beauty alone or what they perceive them to be internally. Stalkers always want something from the victim they stalk, whether it's sex, a reaction of fear, romance or murder.

At the opposite end of the spectrum of both is, for example, a serial killer who becomes highly unpredictable on what a gift like flowers represents. I also told the bartender this secret admirer could be a violent man as well. It would be uncommon for a serial killer to give a gift of flowers unless it was used to lure his victim. Flowers are too personal. The killer usually doesn't wish to get socially attached to his victim because he doesn't want to alter his fantasy. Hence, he needs to keep himself emotionally isolated from his targeted victim so his fantasies continue to dictate accordingly with the way he perceives the victim's reality. The killer makes up his own story about his victim's reality. Hence, the blueprint of his victim's life is edited by the killer into his own image of what his fantasies represent.

Before the killer is geared up to kill there's something about his intended victim that makes her easier to kill. Easy, meaning in the light of revenge and sexual purpose. If the killer gets emotionally involved with the victim his fantasies become void and it makes the victim more difficult to kill. The reason for this is, if you take the killer out of his emotional element then the victim is detached from the story he has created about his or her life.

If a serial killer did send flowers to the bartender's girlfriend then it would very likely represent the direct opposite of beauty, sharing and growth. The flowers serve as a cover-up to either lure the victim or disguise his personality. The flowers themselves may have no meaning at all. However, the delivery itself does. For example, the person who makes the delivery takes the place of the killer. He sees how easy it is to get to her. In this case the stalker is out of context with reality and exists in a dream state. Hence, he imagines what it would be like to be at the doorstep of his potential victim. He could imagine the look on her face when he delivers his message.

The killer thinks she would be very happy to receive flowers. At first, he perceives she might think they're from her boyfriend. When she finds out they're not she has a good idea of who it could be. She opens the card and sees it's not from either. She begins to wonder as to who it is. It's the wonder that keeps the stalker satisfied.

If a serial killer delivers flowers or any other type of gift including nasty letters, then he is likely to attack in the same manner the gift was presented in order to generate the same response from his victim. For instance, think of yourself giving or receiving a gift from another person. When you give a gift you find pleasure and satisfaction of placing the gift in that person's hands. The greatest joy is from the person's reaction after they open up your gift. Why? You put a lot of time and effort into planning and picking out the right gift. Most of all, you picked the right moment to give your gift. The stalker finds the precise moment to give his gift. The first few minutes of giving and receiving this gift are crucial. The person receiving the gift is in suspense and the stalker enjoys every minute of it. Once the gift is opened, he or she no longer looks for facial expressions because the suspense is over. Hence, the same concept exists in dealing with the killer's method of attack and the moment of attack on the victim itself.

The first few seconds of the attack are crucial. The killer picks the precise moment to strike. He picks the time and the place not only for safety reasons but also to relive the fantasy. The victim's facial expressions during the initial attack will be sexually gratifying for the killer. Hence, the stalker stops stalking when he gets what he wants and it becomes too boring to continue.

Before and during the attack, which can sometimes last up to a few minutes, the killer is left in suspense. He is unaware of how his victim will react to his approach versus the attack itself. He's constructed fantasies about what could happen or what should happen when he attacks. Again, before the killer's approach there's a story created about his victim that's usually sexually motivated. His story is created and consistent to the desired reaction of his victim during the attack. This is why the killer attempts to use the same method of approach when an item is delivered during the stalking phase. He doesn't want his fantasy to be significantly altered. Hence, he attempts to make his fantasy as real as possible by approaching the victim strategically and consistently with the thought processes he's formed during the initial time he stalked the victim. For example, hate may constitute a delivery of nasty letters, confusion may result in a delivery of a disorganized letter, and so on.

The stalker glares at his victim amidst all the confusion. He creates images of her own reactions as she receives the killer's gift in her hands. Perhaps the flowers are a plot to kill the bartender's girlfriend without warning? It's obvious the stalker picked this girl for a reason. He picked her out of a crowd of many beautiful young women. We have to find what this girl means to the stalker. Meaning provides insight into the stalker's identity. Hence, serial killers may follow a pattern of stalking their prey.

Methodical serial killers tend to stalk their victims before they strike. A methodical serial killer is difficult to catch because of his unpredictability. Ted Bundy is the most notorious example of them all. Non-discriminatory serial killers are more impulsive and use far less stalking procedures. Hence, both methodical and non-discriminatory serial killers are somewhat unpredictable. However, non-discriminatory serial killers tend to follow a pattern. The methodical serial killers or stalkers tend to be more intelligent than the non-discriminatory killers. Usually both types have no connection to the victim. If you dig hard enough there's always a connection that lies beneath the surface. Usually a killer chooses a person for some reason, whether it's for attention, revenge, sexual, or to become something more powerful than humanity.

Again, the methodical serial killer's patterns are far more difficult to uncover than the non-discriminatory patterns. However, understanding both types can be rather difficult. The answers sometimes lie in the realms of stalking.

Chapter XVIII
RESEARCH PERSPECTIVES I

What's the definition of a serial killer? Different sources stipulate various criteria. For example, the Federal Bureau of Investigation describes a serial killer as one who kills "three or more times, as separate events with an emotional cooling-off period between homicides." (*Journal of Forensic Science*, Volumes 1 and 52)

The National Institute of Justice (NIJ) defines serial murder as "a series of two or more murders committed as separate events, usually with the offender acting alone." (*Journal of Forensic Science*, Volumes 2 and 53)

Serial murder has recently developed into a popular phenomenon, and continues to be a hot topic of discussion, particularly brought on by the media.

The FBI maintains an official listing of the nation's male and female serial killers based on the information from police reports submitted nationwide, as well as from regular computer searches of newswire services. "Using the FBI definition, The National Center of The Analysis of Violent Crime has identified 331 serial murderers in the United States alone, between 1977 and 1992." (Vernon J Gerberth, MS, MPS, Ronald Turco, MD)

What do these numbers and definitions mean? We are such a unique species in that we derive satisfaction in categorizing and classifying almost everything, including violence and those who act on its behalf. We use certain languages in our definition of violence to form complex similarities that include or exclude certain information or to ascertain the truth of its disposition. Language is used everyday on the battlefield in the courtrooms of America. For intensive purposes, language and definitions can either persuade a judge or a jury towards the essence of guilt and innocence, or freedom and incarceration.

The previous statistics are probably gross underestimates. With credit to some state and federal law enforcement agencies, approximately one-third of all serial killers, serial rapists and general murderers have been caught. This means approximately two-thirds of all serial killers, serial rapists and regular unsolved murders, or what the FBI refers to as UNSUBs (unidentified subjects), are currently at large.

Despite the myth that serial murders are confined only to the United States is a big misconception. It's true the United States has the most serious problem with these types of offenders. However, countries like Canada, Great Britain, Germany, Australia and Russia have their own scattered cases of serial murder. Unfortunately, their law enforcement techniques and training aren't equipped enough to deal with this type of criminal. In extreme cases, the FBI's Behavioral Science Unit in Quantico, Virginia is called on internationally to assist in apprehending the unknown suspect.

Research continues to show that one of the underlying motivations for serial killers is the essence of the thrill of the kill and the power they receive over the victim. Moreover, most serial killers gain profound satisfaction from total domination and control over the life of their victim. We will discuss more of this aspect in later chapters. For now, I'll jump into some of the statistics based on the primary motivations for serial killings. Research has shown that one of the primary motivations for serial killers is brought on sexually, or related to unspecified sexual deviance. This includes but is not limited to the sexual act itself, but the act and the sexual inadequacies mask themselves in the forms of rape, masturbation, object insertion, digital penetration, and so on. These acts of sexual fantasy are suppressed early on, in youth and begin to express themselves, pathologically, in the present.

They may be expressed in the form of paraphilias or

personal/unspecified types of sexual deviancies and patterns of behavior. Please note: their apparent behavior based on the sexual crime is expressed in forms of masturbation. Most likely you'll find their technique is carried out in non-traditional means.

In 1997, I interviewed an inmate in prison who used to masturbate in his closet and then ejaculate on his cat. After studying the case and speaking with the inmate I hypothesized the motivations of his masturbatory techniques. His technique and thought process had developed early, during childhood and continued throughout adolescence. What was even more interesting was the story he created and relived after he murdered his first victim.

Reportedly, the inmate pretended he was in a dungeon with a beautiful girl (his victim) whom he had just met at a party. An unidentified creature that the inmate sketched on a piece of paper presented himself as a well-groomed attractive man. The girl (victim) was subsequently lured by the creature into a deserted building and he sank his teeth into her neck and then ate her.

In this case, the closet represents the dungeon and the cat represents the creature in the fantasy. Hence, the girl turned out to be his sister and the creature was his stepfather. Reportedly, the inmate's stepfather forced him to have sex when he was eleven years old with his nine-year-old sister.

Indeed, my theory on the inmate is debatable. However masturbatory techniques can reveal the glimmer of an unyielding mask that portrays some of the underlying motivational factors behind the nature of extreme violence.

Chapter XIX
RESEARCH PERSPECTIVES II

The concept of psychopathy is thought to be integral to the personality structure of a serial murderer. However, I believe psychopathy does not provide a relevant explanation into the mind of a serial killer. This concept has been brought on by the public in order to establish some sense of understanding, in that they are different from us, as normal human beings. Research has continuously shown that most serial killers are not the product of major mental illness, but make a conscious choice in committing their crimes against humanity.

The only psychopathology that exists in serial killers is one that separates them from society's cultural and social norms. Meaning, it's against the customs of most societies to kill innocent people at random.

Research has shown that serial killers tend to have personality disorders such as antisocial personality disorder, or multiple personality disorder, and may also be suffering from sexual disorders, such as erectile dysfunction, premature ejaculation or some sort of paraphilia. A small percentage of them have been diagnosed with a major mental illness like paranoid schizophrenia and some serial killers have been found to have an organic brain syndrome.

Since most serial murders have a sexual orientation attached to their crime, it's likely that most serial killers have some sort of sexual dysfunction, paraphilia, or personality disorder. Although it's difficult to prove, some serial killers are known to have at least some organic brain damage. Many times mild brain damage goes undiagnosed but its element of truth lies at the core of invisible neurotransmitter function.

For example, certain transmitter substances manipulate our behavior via pathways that lead to the brain. When there is a substantial increase or decrease of these substances, it can initiate or decrease certain behaviors.

Some research has shown that serial killers disassociate themselves from their actions. I don't necessarily believe this is true. For one, the telltale data from this research was compiled during the serial killer's captivity. We really do not have any data on serial killers functioning in their natural environment. We only know from what they tell us and our observations of the mess they leave behind. If serial killers disassociated themselves from their actions they wouldn't continue to develop a genuine taste for killing.

It is possible that serial killers detach themselves from reality in an effort to endure specific aspects of their fantasy. For example, serial killers may disassociate themselves from the actual kill but they do not disconnect themselves from the victim's actions and facial expressions, before and during the kill. After the kill, they may disassociate themselves for a while until they decide to kill again. Hence, their detachment from the reality of the kill places them in a comfort zone making it easier for them to kill the next time. This example may be one explanation of why some serial killers become better as time goes by.

Chapter XX
IN THE LINE OF FIRE

Research has concluded that a great many serial killers are obsessed with pornographic materials. Many have been found to steal women's clothing or masturbate with women's underwear. Many have also been found to exhibit voyeuristic activities such as peeking through windows while a woman undresses or stalking. A smaller percentage of serial killers engage in sadomasochistic bondage, frotteurism (rubbing against animate or inanimate objects), obscene phone calls, coprophilia (fascination with feces), and urophilia (fascination with urine).

What hasn't been examined in detail is the different types, or mixtures of pornographic materials, how they relate to each serial killer and the underlying aspects of his crime and finally, the impact of these materials on the mindset of a serial killer. The magazines may start out as *Playboy*, but they work their way into the dirty smut magazines. The smut magazines I'm referring to contain naked pictures of women being tied up, beaten, strangled, and having foreign objects inserted into their vaginal region.

The difference between magazines like *Playboy* and *Smut Fever* is that one shows its potential for sensuality and passion. The other displays women as merely sex objects, while the women's facial expressions in these magazines express hatred and a desire to be sadistically raped and tortured. These are the magazines I'll concentrate on the most because they're the ones that may precipitate a serial killer or serial rapist's anger and hatred towards women.

A serial murderer who masturbates and fantasizes about the

women in these smut magazines wishes to bring them to life. The more time he spends masturbating and fantasizing about these women the more he wishes to experience a sexual relationship with them. It comes to a point where all he can think about are the women in the magazines and the pain they willingly seek.

He views the women in the magazine as objects of desire with no feeling of emotion. His fantasy includes total control and domination of these women. Hence, the killer's victim in some sense represents the women in these smut magazines. This is why it is important not to rule out a serial murder suspect's pornographic materials.

If the serial killer's motive is sexual, which most of the time it is, masturbation material is a vital part of the ongoing investigation, besides providing an insight into the serial killer's thought process.

I've come across a case related to murder and pornography. This man was definitely one of the more interesting inmates I've interviewed. He was a twenty-nine-year-old successful truck driver, serving a life sentence for the murder of a young girl. To understand his story and the state of mind he was in, at the time of the murder, he asked me to imagine the scenario that led up to what he did.

He said, "Christ, I'm a truck driver and I'm always on the road. I'm on the road quite a bit so I didn't have much contact with my family, let alone any beautiful women. Boy, would I ever have loved to meet a woman that day I killed her. I parked my truck on the side of the road and opened up my first issue of *Playboy* magazine. I'm thinking to myself these women are so beautiful and sexy. How bad do I want these women in the magazine? Bad enough to masturbate in your front seat."

Believe it or not, this is how it all happened for this inmate. Continue to imagine this truck driver's scenario as your own. After you masturbate to the *Playboy* magazine, you're probably shuffling through the magazine, trying to decide what woman you want and what you would do if you had her. Perhaps you're thinking of marriage, a honeymoon in Las Vegas, a private cruise to a deserted island where you can have sex all day. Nevertheless, when reality hits you with the fact that you have a wife and two kids at home, you're spellbound for words. You've been driving this truck for eighteen hours and feel depressed and frustrated about your current situation in life. You masturbate to the woman in *Playboy* because she makes you feel comfortable. It bothers you sometimes that your life can't be better and you're starting to hate your job. Also, you're not attracted to your wife anymore. She doesn't like to have that kinky sex you love.

A week goes by and a friend on the road gives you a smut and bondage magazine to look at for the first time. This looks a lot different from the other magazines you're used to masturbating to. The women in this magazine aren't as good-looking and passionate compared to the girls you're used to seeing in *Playboy*. These women are holding guns to guys' heads. You're in a lousy mood again and thinking about your lousy job and lousy wages.

You continue to find pleasure in masturbating to the women in the smut magazine. You enjoy masturbating to the smut magazine because it coincides with how you're feeling about life. You just want to find this type of women in the magazine and "rail" them hard. You don't want a relationship with these women at all. Looking at them pose in this magazine, you think they're filthy and disgusting.

You've been on the road for about a month and have masturbated to the smut magazines for about three weeks. Then one night in a motel you decide to masturbate with the *Playboy* magazine instead of the smut magazine. It's been a few weeks, but guess what the truck driver is fantasizing about?

Maybe you guessed it? The truck driver's "visionary fantasy" is being projected or transformed from the thoughts of the women in the smut magazine onto the women in the *Playboy* magazine. He no longer views the women in the *Playboy* as sensual, passionate, beautiful and sexy. Instead, they're posing as filthy objects just like the sluts in the smut magazine.

The truck driver is beginning to look more at their bodies instead of their faces. Hence, he's perceiving their internal expressions of desire as external expressions of hate and physical pain. Additionally, he's beginning to have fantasies about inflicting physical pain on women. His thought patterns and subsequent behavior is consistent with the visual stimulus (smut magazines). In other words, he's projecting his own feelings of hate and his desire for physical pain onto the women in the magazine.

Two months pass and the truck driver arrives home. He is confused and frustrated about his job, family, boss, and lack of sex in his marriage. He wants more of a sexual variety, and these fantasies begin to consume his thoughts. He's masturbating more often than usual and he's using the beautiful girls he looks at on the road, as various masturbating tools.

At rest stops, he begins stalking pretty young girls wearing shorts and imagines what it would be like to rape them. This particular person has a thigh fetish. The truck driver glares at a beautiful young teenage girl wearing shorts. All the while he's picturing what it would be like to rape this young girl. Hence, he processes the vision in his brain of the girl's body, particularly her legs so he can masturbate later.

At this point the truck driver's thought processes are beginning to scatter from "normal" thoughts to disorganized and violent thoughts. However, at this point he's not acting on behalf of his thoughts. Hence, he's still functioning within normal limits.

However, he's fantasizing and masturbating on a sadistic level. It eventually comes to a point where the truck driver's only means for maintaining control and relief is through masturbation.

The truck driver's fantasizing and masturbating more about the young girls he sees at the restaurants and rest stops. A few times he even spoke to a couple of young girls at one of the restaurants located just off the highway. He said to one of the girls, "Hey, how's it goin' today?" Her response was, "Fine", and she walked away from him. Usually, if he tried to strike up any conversations with girls on the road at bars and restaurants they wouldn't give him the time of day. In other words, they just stonewalled him and walked away. This behavior confirms the truck driver's notion that he's worthless and not worthy of getting intimate with a pretty girl. Hence, the more the truck driver is rejected by women unknown to him just like in the magazine, the more it perpetuates his feelings of anger and low self-worth. It also perpetuates the truck driver's hostile feelings towards his wife and now other women as well.

After the extreme avoidance behavior demonstrated by the women, coupled with his deviant sexual arousal patterns, it becomes apparent that he's beginning to think about doing something negative. Hence, he carries the thoughts that all the beautiful women he looks at and masturbates to in the *Playboy* and smut magazines are alike.

This is dangerous because the truck driver is classifying all women in a negative sphere. Hence, he's masturbating to the thoughts of inflicting pain on the women he encounters at restaurants and bars. At this point in time it takes one stressful event to push the truck driver over the edge.

Masturbating to a magazine is all it takes for a disturbed person to change his course of thinking and behavior towards women. Under extreme circumstances the most perverse thinking will be put into action. For example, just a few more bad encounters with women and the loss of something important can push a man such as the truck driver over the edge.

After several months of rejection coupled with stress the truck driver's fantasies graduate from rape to torture. For now his masturbatory technique and visionary fantasy is completely facilitated through pornographic magazines. However, he's starting to ignore the magazines and concentrate on the strangers he sees in restaurants, bars and hotels. Instead of the truck driver's deviant sexual fantasies being subdued to inanimate objects in the pornographic magazines, he now seeks live objects as targets of masturbation.

Five months have passed since the truck driver first masturbated to the smut magazines his friend gave him. During that extensive timeframe in between he's managed to acquire quite a collection of *Playboy*, *Club Confidential* and *Penthouse* magazines. We all agree that he has a solid amount of masturbatory materials.

Another week passes and the truck driver loses his job. He's continuously arguing with his wife and he's very angry about a phone bill he just received. It seems his wife has been calling a man long-distance for quite some time.

Feeling angry, deceived and rejected again, he takes off from the house and goes for a long drive. He's been driving for a couple hours now until he eventually decides to pull off the highway at a rest stop. He sees a beautiful girl in her late teens heading towards the women's bathroom.

He recalls the whole time watching this girl and saying to himself, "There's no way this girl would ever want me". He said to himself, "This girl looks like one of these typical girls I've been masturbating to. I don't know which one, because they all look alike."

The truck driver gets out of his truck and heads to the bathroom. He checks the men's room and then yells inside the lady's room. Nobody was in the women's bathroom except for the teenage girl. The girl's family was waiting outside for her.

Her family waited longer than usual before finally realizing their daughter's fate. The young girl was brutally raped and murdered by the hands of the truck driver I've been speaking about. The truck driver had time to rape her, kill her, bury her and the next day go look for a job.

The girl's body was discovered three weeks later by joggers thirty-five miles from where she was abducted. Apparently, the truck driver struck the victim's head against the bathroom wall as she was coming out of the bathroom. The victim's bloodstains were on the walls in the bathroom as evidence at the crime scene. There were no screams or any signs of a struggle. The whole thing happened instantaneously. According to investigative reports the girl didn't stand a chance. The unsuspecting victim was an eighteen-year-old freshman in college. Her hobbies were dance, computers and art. She had always wanted to study medicine in college.

The first thing that comes to mind in this case is the truck driver beginning to lose control of his life. He essentially lost it just before he killed the young girl. Even though the truck driver feels remorse for what he did he always recalls how calm he felt just after he murdered this girl. He quotes, "I felt a serenity on the road that I've never felt before. It's as if I disappeared from everyone and everything."

Losing his job was a trigger to violence. Hence, he used it as an excuse to rape and murder the girl. To the truck driver's credit his initial intention wasn't to kill the girl. His intentions were to control and manipulate her into having sex with him. It's as if he used the girl to gain control over his own life at that very moment.

The sexual gesture of the act itself is the victim's symbolic representation of the perpetrator's wish for control over his life. One of these components includes but is not limited to the alleged fact that the truck driver's wife refused to adhere to his sexual wishes. As a result the perpetrator decided to fulfill his sexual fantasies elsewhere on someone (the victim) or something else, such as the smut magazines.

Once he finished raping the victim he planned on letting her go. However, she continued to struggle so he had to kill her. He was also frightened that she would tell her parents and authorities.

Fortunately, the killer was apprehended by local police before he was given a chance to strike again. Although the truck driver was never labeled a serial killer he potentially could have been. If given the chance he would've killed again because of the relief and sense of satisfaction it gave him the first time.

Chapter XXI

A SEARCH FOR AN ANSWER

There was once a story I heard that someone babysat a child who many years later butchered seven people including a ninety-year-old lady. Can you imagine coming across a child in a supermarket who'll someday become a serial killer? Who knows, maybe the child next to you will someday fit that mold? One thing is for certain, that we cannot predict violence twenty years down the road. It's important that we as a society understand this and live by it.

We all want to know what happened to convicted serial killers when they were small children. The passion for us to know is so great that we've devised standardized testing procedures in an attempt to categorize and predict violent behavior. Most of the compiled research comes directly from the serial killers themselves.

What has been found in testing procedures and subsequent research is correlations between physical child abuse and neglect. However, there is no validity to predict extreme violent behavior in the future as a result of physical abuse or neglect during childhood.

Still, the majority of sadistic behavior is attributed to childhood abuse. In many cases, it has been found that sadistic behavior has existed in the serial killers' childhood history. Research has shown that early aggressive behavior of serial killers is first acted out on animals and then, later on, with smaller children. In essence, research shows that sexual aggression becomes a patterned response and is established within the child's mind. It becomes reinforced in ritualistic play with children of their own peers.

The problem is that sexual aggression covers a broad spectrum having an endless continuum. Hence, varying behavior in children can be deemed as sexually aggressive or acting out. For example, if a child plays with certain toys accompanying another child the toys can arguably represent phallic symbols. Also, a sadistic child can play aggressively with another child without either child realizing their intentions. For example, a child may wrestle or concentrate on a particular body part of another child without recognizing his intention of gathering visionary material for later masturbation.

Neither the child receiving the pain nor the child giving it realizes his intentions. All that the children know is that they enjoy playing with each other and wish to continue.

Masturbation in early childhood is manifested through aggressive child-play. It isn't until early adolescence that the potential serial killer begins to use his genitalia during masturbation. His masturbatory techniques and fantasies are likely to remain consistent throughout adolescence and into adulthood.

Additional research in 1986 on serial killers has shown that many are a product of dysfunctional families and have experienced some sort of childhood violence. Studies have shown that many serial killers come from alcohol or drug abusing environments as well. Also many have a history of mental illness in the family and had parents who were themselves participants in criminal activity. The results of this research should not be much of a surprise for the culmination of a criminal mind is modeled on those we trust and confide in. Please keep in mind that most of the extensive research on serial killers has been conducted many years ago.

Since then a lot has changed. New types of serial killers have entered the market and their motives have become even more mysterious. For example, Ted Bundy was allegedly brought up in a stable environment. However, it was later discovered Ted may have suffered from some sort of emotional abuse by his mother.

Most serial killers who have been abused, come from families of alcoholics, and their families as well as themselves have had a history of mental illness. We mention these things because it makes us feel more comfortable classifying serial killers as anything but normal. The truth is what we know about serial killers comes directly from the FBI. How do you think the FBI knows about these guys?

The FBI's elite Behavioral Resource Unit in Quantico, Virginia, interviews incarcerated serial killers and conducts research on the information provided by the inmates themselves. The information is gathered and placed into an organized index. After careful analysis and interpretation we come up with a universal character-logical profile on serial killers. Is it accurate? The answer is sometimes yes. Remember, we have to consider the source of our information. It comes straight from the serial killers themselves. How much of it is true depends on who is telling the story and the motivation they have in telling it. Hence, we have to rely on the information they provide us during these interviews. Remember, most serial killers are known to be the most cunning and manipulative antisocial personalities of all.

What makes them so effective in the art of manipulation is their own genuineness and belief in their own cahn (lies). Most serial killers lie unintentionally or confabulate in order to appreciate themselves for what they have done. Confabulation doesn't only apply to serial killers. In other words, outside of serial killers, expert manipulators and liars become good at their trade because they believe in their own lies. Hence, this tactic helps us get what we want. In the serial murderer's case it makes him more of an efficient hunter.

Chapter XXII

SERIAL MURDERERS AS SADISTS

Serial killers do not necessarily become sexual sadists and sexual sadists are not necessarily serial killers. The fine line between them both occurs when one supersedes the other. For example, a pre-existing sexual sadist becomes a serial murderer by killing his victims for sexual pleasure, and vice versa. Hence, the term "lust murderer".

In previous chapters we've mentioned that most serial murderers kill in order to fulfill some internal fantasy that's manifested primarily by sexual means. How can one find sexual pleasure in murder? To answer this question we have to go beyond the act of murder itself. It's not the act of violence that sexually stimulates the killer, it's the time before and after the murder takes place. Hence, most serial killers who are sexual sadists have either a physiological sexual disorder, such as premature ejaculation and paraphilias, such as fetishism.

There has been extensive research on paraphilias in connection with serial murderers. Sexual sadism is a compelling element in most lust murderers, in others the arousal does not take place from the infliction of pain and the suffering of the victim but rather on the act of violence. Lust murderers are known to relive the kill over and over again. Many times they manipulate the actual scene or what happened on the victim during the attack. Again, this calls on the imagination of the killer in order to satisfy his original fantasy.

If the serial killer's fantasy is not fulfilled either before, during or after his initial attack on the victim, which most of the time it isn't, then he will fill in the missing parts during the attack as he mirrors his victims through the fear in their eyes. A sexual sadist must inflict physical pain on the victim in order to sexually stimulate himself. Hence, there is no before or after.

The lust murderer will very likely masturbate in the form of his diagnosed paraphilia or mental condition. For example, an organized killer who happens to be a necrophiliac (sexual attraction to dead bodies) will probably masturbate when he gets home and not at the scene of the crime. When he arrives at a safe distance and waits the following day he will envision the dead body as he last saw him/her.

Organized serial killers who are necrophiliacs will, very likely, leave the corpse undressed. The reason is because necrophiliacs are likely to have some type of fetish to go along with the paraphilia. Hence, the fetish is connected with a specific body part to go along with his sexual attraction for dead bodies; for example, the killer may have a foot fetish, a leg fetish, a back fetish. Hence, the corpse must remain naked in order to satisfy both his back fetish and the attraction to dead bodies.

The primary method for sexual stimulation for lust murderers is to leave their victims undressed so that they can masturbate at a later time and place. Sometimes these guys bring video cameras or Polaroids to the scene of the crime. Additionally, they may take jewelry or pictures of the victim, including her identification card. Hence, these items as well as the pictures are used for the sole purposes of masturbation and bringing the crime back to life. Finally, a lust murderer with some sort of paraphilia may select an occupation or have a hobby bringing him in to closer contact with the desired stimuli of the paraphilia; for example, one who has a woman's foot fetish may desire employment in a woman's shoe store.

We've discussed aspects of an organized lust murderer. Now let's turn our attention to an unorganized serial lust murderer. Unlike an organized lust murderer, an unorganized lust murderer will probably masturbate at the scene of the crime and leave the victim undressed, or even both. An organized lust murderer is less likely to take a chance in masturbating at the scene of the crime because he's much more effective in evaluating the high risk of getting caught.

Unorganized lust murderers may have varying symptoms of a paraphilia mixed with some type of psychotic symptoms. Hence, they usually have poor judgment and will attack during the daytime if the opportunity presents itself. Unlike the organized lust murderer these guys are likely to rape and murder in shorter increments. Consequently, they are a bit easier to catch than the organized offender because they tend to ignore the risk attached to their crime. Organized lust murderers will at times spread out their attacks over time and attempt to throw off authorities by altering the disposal of the body. An organized serial lust murderer may stage a homicide every now and then to make it look like an accident or somebody else has committed the crime.

Both the organized and unorganized lust murderers feed off a similar modus operandi that is primarily sexual in nature. Hence, most of them have suffered from some sort of childhood physical, sexual or emotional abuse.

One of the inmates I interviewed fell into the category of an unorganized lust murderer. His mother disappeared when he was three years old and his father was in prison for twenty years for second-degree murder. At one of the foster homes this inmate was sexually abused and beaten almost on a daily basis. He said that it wasn't until he was a teenager that he started having violent sexual fantasies towards women. There was one "precipitating" event in his life that pushed this man over the edge into violence and "lust murder".

We refer to lust murderers as serial killers if they intend to kill more victims over time and have a relative "cooling-off period" in between murders. If their intent is not to kill then we refer to them as rapists. In the upcoming chapters we'll discuss the theories of rape and the types of rapists who commit the act.

Chapter XXIII

THEORIES OF RAPE

I want my readers to close their eyes for ten seconds. Pick four women who you love and care about. Open your eyes when you have picked the four women. Statistics show that at least one, out of the four women, will be raped during your lifetime.

What is rape? The dictionary definition and its terminology explains the act itself. It's forcible seizing, violation and ravishing. I'll spare you most of the research on rape such as power and control and focus on why rapists want to establish this power and control. What is their perception of power and control?

Would it surprise you that for some rapists sexual gratification comes not from the intercourse itself but the reaction of the victim before he initiates it? The reason is because in some instances a male rapist doesn't establish control over his victim within the first seconds of the attack. However, he perceives control before he attacks. Hence, he wants to get a glimpse of the victim while she's in her resting state just before he engages in his attack.

The rapists I'll discuss in this section are what the FBI's Behavioral Resource Unit refers to as "anger-based rapists" and "power-based rapists". Power-based rapists are the men who pre-select their victims. These people do all the stalking, and they wait for the right time and place to attack. Hence, they search extensively for the right victim. However, like the anger-based rapists, they later become opportunistic hunters.

The power-based rapist's motives are primarily sexually based. For example, date rape falls into this category. One of the primary motives for date rape is to re-establish control; control of your life as well as control over the victim. The rapist's sense of control overlaps his sense of power-reassurance. For example, he has to feel powerful in order to feel in control, and vice versa.

In certain instances date rape falls into the category of anger-based rape. In order for the rape to be anger-based there must be a significant stressor leading to the attack itself, and it's usually not manifested in sexual terms. For example, you just broke up with a girlfriend and you have a rocky family situation. Either situation can precipitate into extreme violence during a rape that is motivated by such stress. As such, in an anger-based rape the victim is usually hospitalized.

Power-based rapists usually have low self-esteem and indulge in rape to fulfill their crippled self-image. If during or after the rape the victim fulfills the rapist's needs then the power-based rapist will feel sorry for his victim. Hence, he'll attempt to establish an ongoing relationship with her by sending her flowers, love letters, and such like.

Anger-based rapists are likely to stalk their victims just as their counterparts except they tend to be a lot less picky. The one thing that sets power-based and anger-based rapists apart from one another is that anger-based rapists, by their nature, have little or no remorse after the rape occurs. Hence, their victim is usually physically harmed, bruised, beaten and can even have dangerous objects inserted into her genitalia.

The anger-based rapist's primary motive is dominated by anger and facilitated through serial fantasy. His feelings of anger manifest themselves by either unconscious or conscious sexually sadistic fantasies. For example, an anger-based rapist may select a beautiful young woman because he was rejected by one in the past or just the other day. In this case his motive for rape is conscious. However, he may not realize his sadistic need to inflict harm on the victim.

I recall speaking to a convicted serial rapist on the telephone in a maximum-security prison outside of Denver,

Colorado. We spoke for fifteen minutes and I remember one of the things he said to me was, "I saw her first; why not rape her? She wouldn't have sex with me anyway." I determined this was an anger-based rapist because of his comment. He thought the victim wouldn't want him, so he took it upon himself to take her. Anger-based rapists and power-based rapists tend to have low self-esteem but primarily they're "pissed off".

Issues of the anger-based rapist go deeper than feelings of loss, frustration, anger and rejection. Some issues are even manifested in early childhood and fueled by precipitating events that occur in the present. For example, you lose your job, you're in the midst of a divorce, or a woman rejects you.

Depending on how the victim reacts in accordance with the anger-based rapist's fantasy is likely to determine the severity of the rape itself. Unfortunately, there's no universal answer in acting appropriately or inappropriately during the time you're confronted and attacked by either a power-based or an anger-based rapist. It depends on the individual attacker and what's going through his mind during the attack. Hence, we don't know for how long and how intensely the development of violent tendencies escalated before he reached this point; for example, what's motivating the rapist who chose you.

If you've read the previous chapter up to this point you may have ideas on how to react if you happen to encounter a rapist. I spoke to my colleague at work and she told me if she was ever attacked by an anger-based rapist she would go into complete submission. I asked her why. "Because if he's been rejected his whole life he expects his victim to bite and kick him when he attacks. If I do the opposite I may get away from the rapist alive." I must caution my readers as I did my colleague. There's no absolute advice on how to react when confronted by a rapist. Some reactions may or may not work with either an anger-based or power-based rapist. However, if one evening you encounter an anger-based rapist and you follow the advice of my colleague, you may find the rapist gets even more angry because he perceives his victim's submissive behavior as an attempt to trick him.

Most experts do believe it is very dangerous to offer confrontational advice, mainly because the human mind is so complex you cannot possibly have only one answer to it all. You must take into consideration, certain aspects of the perpetrator's motives for his attack, the time of the day and the personality profile of the hypothetical victim. Again, extensive research shows that there is no absolute way to deal with a rape situation.

Obviously, the advice one would provide someone who's attacked at noon in a parking lot of a drug store is different compared to someone who's attacked at an overnight dwelling at 3:00 A.M. More people are likely to be around the parking lot of a drugstore and the act would be more impulsive, and of course, riskier. So you are probably dealing with an unstable rapist. If you are attacked at an overnight dwelling at 3:00 A.M., the rapist is likely to be more methodical but can still be unstable.

Based on the research and motivation of law enforcement officers the best advice is none at all. However, it would be beneficial to attend law enforcement workshops and seminars to perhaps understand the dynamics of the two different types of rapists we have discussed, their motivations and, most of all, the dangers of giving any confrontational advice.

Chapter XXIV

CONFRONTATIONS OF MAN

To exist within the boundaries of technology is to lie within the mouth of madness. This sentence describes the future of mental illness and its effects on the world. If you recall when Europe hit its industrial revolution, America was further developing its wits in the technological arena. Hence, during this time fierce competition existed between man and machine. There was a tussle between who could build the fastest ship, see the orbiting planets, or build the smartest bomb. Competition between countries spread to man himself.

The traditional family is but a memory in the midst of technological growth and advancement. Children from one-parent homes learn the value of change as the essence of life. For change is what brought the child to his/her present state of existence. Hence, change is what separated his/her parents. Finally, change brings about progress and progress sets forth competition. Today, more and more people suffer from stress and mental illnesses. The interesting question is how and where did all this begin?

The industrial revolution brought about new advances in media and telecommunications. The advent of radio and television swept across the United States and Europe, bringing sitcoms of make believe humor, drama and fantasy to life. It wasn't until recently that we began glorifying the aspects of violence. Today we are a society and culture that accepts violence in our daily repertoire. Hence, we are intrigued by its nature and subsequent development.

Let's look at entertainment in our society, especially sports. Almost every popular American and European sport is violent.

Football and hockey are the more obvious sports that facilitate violence. Surprisingly, baseball, tennis, golf and soccer have their roots of violence as well. For example, in tennis we use a racket to hit a tennis ball over the net as hard as we can. Who is the racket and who is the ball? Golf has a similar connection with violence. We use a golf club to drive a golf ball about five hundred yards. The pitchers in baseball throw a ball as hard as they can towards another person holding a glove. It just so happens that before the ball arrives there's someone with a bat trying to hit the hell out of it.

We do not refer to this as violence because no physical harm is done on another person. Hence, this type of violence is controlled for the most part. However, some of these sports have aggressive tendencies that may or may not lead to violence. This statement is not only true for professional athletes, but it's true for everyone who encounters stressful events in his/her life.

We all have the same aggressive tendencies but we have different thresholds or breaking points that lead to violence. Hence, some people are better than others in finding acceptable means of releasing their anger. Unfortunately, some breaking points are shorter than others.

Some aspects of violence can be facilitated by the media. Look at what happened in Colombine High School in Littleton, Colorado in April 1999. There was non-stop media coverage for approximately two weeks after the shooting resulting in the deaths of fifteen students and one teacher. Not even three weeks afterwards, there were approximately seven bomb threats of schools in Florida across Broward and Dade Counties alone, as well as a school in Atlanta, Georgia. Why do you think this happens? Nobody really knows for certain. However, most of the kids' motives lay within the attention factor. Let me give you another example. How often does the news ever cover something good? Not often and it is saved for the end of the broadcast.

Sometimes even if the news is good there's a negative and

violent connotation to it. For example, in September 1999, in Florida, a young man and his wife, both in their late twenties, were attacked in a hotel by three young men. Little did the attackers know that the victim was an army ranger. Reportedly, he worked the three young men over pretty good. The point is, the media didn't tell us anything about the couple, like the victim and his wife's name, or how long they've lived in Florida. Instead, they just talked about how the victim worked these three teenagers over. What's the one thing this tells us as a society? One of the messages it conveys is that it's okay to take matters into your own hands. There was so much attention focused on the victim that he turned out to be a hero. Young children, adolescents or disoriented adults may look for ways to get the attention the victim did in this case. Unfortunately, people will commit acts of violence on others, particularly in Colorado, to get a rise out of people and to attract attention onto themselves.

The two adolescents accused of the Colombine shooting took their own lives in the process of killing many of their classmates. This was a planned operation of revenge spawned by a general hatred of their classmates. This hatred wasn't directed at any one person. Instead, it was directed towards the dynamics of a system which was indirectly perpetuated by the movies, television, radio, media and the fascination with weaponry.

Something like this would've never happened twenty years ago. During the late eighties and early nineties we haven't seen too much of an increase and decrease in serial and mass murder. Unfortunately, we can expect to see many more mass murderers like the Colombine massacre in the years to come.

Like Colombine, mass murderers use violence as their final attempt in getting their points across to the world. They had their hands out for help a long time ago but they've been ignored. What we see doesn't matter to them. The fact is they perceive they are alone and continue to be ignored. Their last attempt of violence says, "I told you so."

What lies at the root of a mass and serial murder? The answer is something like this: as we enter into the technologically advanced world we are becoming a more productive, competitive and demanding society. Today this philosophy upholds the nature of the American family and its subsequent culture. We view change as a paradigm of natural existence. Within change our children suffer and look to others in establishing meaningful and lasting relationships. We look to our peers, animals, media, movies and the radio to establish intimacy.

We look at these aspects of comfort and entertainment because they soothe our soul. We form wishes and fantasies based on our interpretations of the television and movies we watch, our forms of plays that are make-believe and the music we open our ears to. We're a society based on sensation and perception, reward and punishment, success and failure, and right and wrong.

The core of mankind is violent and our children embrace the nature it was predicated on. Hence, we can expect an increase in all kinds of violent crime such as rape, serial murders, spree murders, and especially mass murders in the next centuries to come, if we last that long.

Chapter XXV

SEXUAL SYMBOLISM AND MURDER

A set of symbols that has meaning to the life extracted from his victim tells the story of his pathology. The knife he uses that sheds the victim's blood, the gun's bullets that pierce the angles of her body, and the hands that succumb her last breath tell the killer's tales of truth. His weapon of destruction is usually the origin of his mental state and the fist of his fury.

If the killer uses a knife on his victim it demonstrates pathological rage, excitement or hyperactivity and a need to be close to his victim and watch it all happen. His fantasy is usually sexual in nature and his mental status is likely unpredictable. Hence, he is complacent, yet impulsive during moments of his life.

The number of stab wounds on the victim both pre- and post-mortem determines the perpetrator's level of rage before, during and after the initial attack itself. The scene of the crime reveals the extent of his anger and sexual fantasy. For instance, excessive arterial spray is likely conducive to the victim's struggle during the attack. Hence, if the crime is sexual in nature the struggle perpetuates the perpetrator's fantasy and he continues to stab his victim to get the desired effect until she stops moving. Hence, in this case the killer "gets off" by the way the victim struggles during the attack. Once the victim stops moving the thrill is over. The killer will likely masturbate at his place of residence if he hasn't at the scene of the crime.

When the killer gathers his thoughts he may or may not have sex with the victim post-mortem. Whether he chooses to or not depends on impulsivity and his personal assessment of risk. A disorganized offender will probably underestimate his risk of being caught and tend to be impulsive. Both organized and disorganized offenders will very likely masturbate at a later time to relive their crime.

The perpetrator's visionary fantasy determines the level and severity of psychosis. For instance, if the perpetrator envisions eating the victim's internal organs and drinking her blood while she is struggling, then he is likely to slip into a more psychotic state along with tendencies of excitement and anger.

If the perpetrator envisions drinking his victim's blood post-mortem then we're dealing with a totally different pathology that can either be more or less intellectually advanced. For example, if the pathology is advanced the perpetrator may believe he's a vampire. In the process he's likely to live the life of a vampire on how he perceives a vampire to be. Hence, he'll likely engage in risky behavior that inevitably may lead to his apprehension. It's this sense of invulnerability that ends most serial killers' crime sprees.

An organized offender would drink his victim's blood post-mortem because he was able to control his behavior to some degree. Hence, the structure of his fantasy is built beyond the attack on the victim itself. For example, it's important for an organized offender to relive his crime.

March 1997 was the year and month that one of the most disturbing cases I've handled landed on my lap. He was a heavy-set man between the age of thirty-two and thirty-eight, serving a life sentence for the murder of a twenty-six-year-old woman he had no relation with. This case was disturbing because what took place during the murder scene was something you don't even see in movies. For what I'm about to tell is not censored. This man broke into the victim's two-bedroom apartment and attacked her with one of those Rambo knives while she was in the kitchen. He stabbed her approximately fourteen times before she was able to run. The victim, bleeding to death, ran into her bedroom and tried to lock the door. The perpetrator was right behind her and before she could get to safety he continued to stab her.

That's not all! In the midst of all the confusion, just before the victim died, the perpetrator put on novelty teeth and proceeded to drink her blood from her neck region. The victim was declared dead at the scene approximately eleven minutes later.

The method of his attack is clearly disorganized. However, he did have organized tendencies. For example, he waited for the right time to attack; for example, he staked out the apartment and waited until the late evening hours as opposed to the early afternoon or early evening hours. Hence, he knew she lived alone and waited until she was ready for bed.

Although at this point this man's plan seems organized because he analyzed his victim's behavior, his plan of attack, however, is completely disorganized. There was no plan. He wasn't supposed to chase his victim around her house. Once he was inside her apartment he had to improvise his next move. His very last move from once he got inside her apartment to her subsequent death was done impulsively. Hence, his behavior both during and immediately after the attack led to his quick apprehension. For instance, the novelty teeth that were used to puncture the victim's neck were quickly traced to a store approximately four miles from where the suspect lived. The clerk in the store identified some man coming into the store but wasn't sure of his answers. He quickly became a suspect and later confessed to killing the young lady himself. Nobody knows why he did it except he indicated that he was jealous of her beauty.

Once a serial killer's preliminary sexual fantasy becomes a reality he'll stop at nothing until he reaches its final goal, which in most cases is total control and domination over his victim. The serial killer's internal fantasies of domination are spread out diffusely across the broad spectrum of his life that predominately manifests itself sexually. Quite simply, the weapon of choice symbolically matches the intent of the killer's sexual prowess.

A bludgeon weapon used at the scene of the crime suggests

that the perpetrator is either angry, resentful, excited, or impatient. The more time the killer has to fantasize about his victim the more violent his attack, hence, the more barbaric the weapon.

For example, an anger-based rapist I spoke to in prison stared at his potential victim in a nightclub for approximately one hour before he decided to strike. The girl was probably eighteen to twenty-one, had several tattoos near her buttocks, blond hair, a slim figure with a voluptuous chest. She wore black tight-fitting pants with a white cut-off T-shirt revealing her slender stomach. She gave the impression that she was able to iron a pair of pants on her.

According to the perpetrator she was dancing alone on the upstairs balcony of the nightclub "very aggressively". He quotes, "She was moving her body rather well to the techno music and grinding up against the railing in the club." The perpetrator approached her and said, "You're a good dancer." She replied almost immediately, "I'm waiting here for my boyfriend so leave me alone." The perpetrator knew she was lying and it angered him even further. At this point he recalled that his anger consumed every part of his body until he imagined how this girl would die. He envisioned stabbing the girl repeatedly while she was lying in her underwear. He could hear her screams and watch her facial expressions until her blood encapsulated the very ground she walked on.

The inmate left the nightclub at around 4:00 A.M. He staked out the nightclub for about an hour until another girl he'd never seen before came out. She was alone and half stumbling from all the alcohol she had consumed. He somehow lured her into his car. Reportedly, she expected to get a ride to her car and that was all. Instead the perpetrator struck her on the head three times with a hammer he kept in his back seat. She was still semi-conscious and that's when he proceeded to strip her all the way down to her underwear. Control was established as the victim lay helplessly drunk and bleeding to death from the head region.

The inmate was angry before he hit the victim over the head with a hammer, but now he's even angrier thinking about the girl who blew him off in the nightclub. Hence, his anger interplayed itself through his sexual fantasy of seeing a girl in her underwear. The perpetrator's feelings of anger, resentment and hate for the girl in the nightclub were projected onto an innocent victim who was just looking for her friends outside a nightclub.

It's stories like these that expand the dangerous depths of fantasies (thoughts) about killing and initiating reality (behavior). We cannot help but be intrigued by the very nature of what makes violent men such as these tick. We can explore the origin and etiology of these men and their separation from good in the presence of evil.

Chapter XXVI

INSPIRATION TO THE BEGINNING

The beginning of time is thought to exist in man's fear for survival. Hence, his fear lies in the evil amidst that which suffocates life.

The proposed aspects of underlying meanings of culture and personality stretch the imagination on the deviations of good versus evil as we enter the world beyond birth.

Just after birth we're unblemished in the sense that no rules apply. It's not until we enter early childhood that we're forced to control the impulsivity of our thoughts. For example, during early childhood we're taught not to urinate and defecate in public places and put certain things inside our mouths. When we get older our every experience impacts on our life.

The developing mind and its thought process, shapes our entire personality structure and the end result of this structure is our common experiences, which exist throughout our entire lives. However, these experiences are most influential during our childhood years. For example, maternal care and economic conditions are a huge part of our internal and external personality development. Hence, our personality structures create the basis for most of our thought patterns. On some occasions we're able to see maladaptive thought patterns develop in early childhood stages. Hence, the way we're raised both physically and mentally, along with our family background and structure, has a strong impact on whether or not we'll develop into sexually maladaptive individuals.

In psychoanalytic theory when we're born it's a traumatic experience because we're forced into a structured way of life.

Hence, according to Freud our id impulses are repressed. Over time our repressed id impulses create a ballooning effect within our system. Hence, we're forced to compensate our previous id-related needs.

As a result of our early traumatic events in withholding id impulses our unique personalities form. Our internal personality structure remains stagnant before we develop into to "secondary aspects of life" that conceal our true need. Essentially, these are our culture's compensatory mechanisms such as religion, art, music, poetry, entertainment and other projective activities that compensate for our primary needs.

What does all this have to do with serial killers? The part where they're concerned is their early traumatic experience of their past has reflected onto the fantasies in the present. For example, the anger and negativity of the perpetrator's past is projected onto their victim in the present. Hence, their victim represents the compensatory mechanism of their id impulse.

Rape and murder are usually unconscious deviant compensatory mechanisms that facilitate the needs of the perpetrator's repressed id impulses. Within these compensatory mechanisms most of us establish norms and morals that govern the rules of our society and culture. The memory structures of the brain establish and implant moralistic values and beliefs which remain culturally specific. The serial killer deviates from this norm and forms his own belief system.

Within the memory structures of the brain lies an invisible mechanism that initiates our behavior based on reality, fantasy, family, environment and cultural experiences. These experiences perpetuate our fantasies and our fantasies perpetuate our experiences. In the serial killer's case his fantasies almost exclusively perpetuate his experience. For example, abusing animals and small children perpetuates a fantasy by making its experience a reality.

Most serial killers coexist in the reality and fantasy modes. Hence, their behavior is facilitated by both spectrums. In the serial killer's case, his fantasy is likely to be sexually maladaptive, and the reality of the serial killer's past and present experiences is repressed only to be discovered through the fantasy mode. Hence, the serial killer usually finds relief in killing people because the invisible mechanism has enhanced his compensatory mechanisms. Hence, it allows him to express his id impulses in a maladaptive manner based on his most difficult past experiences that are initiated in the present.

Chapter XXVII
SERIAL SEXUAL MURDER

Serial murder continues to generate vast intrigue throughout the United States. However, most psychological research and case studies lack a depth of knowledge, differentiating between sexual and non-sexual homicide.

Most of the chapters have been dedicated to serial murder; however, we must differentiate between serial murder with or without a sexual basis. For intensive purposes most serial killers are serial sexual killers.

According to the FBI, approximately four to five thousand Americans each year may be victims of serial killers. The FBI calculates there are approximately thirty-five of these killers operating in the United States alone. However, many criminologists suggest that this is a gross underestimate. One of the reasons for this is because many of the victims' bodies are still missing and a great number of missing persons are essentially homicide victims. Remarkably only three states in the US have not been victimized by serial killers and they are Hawaii, Maine and Iowa. Again this could be because of the difficulties in locating decomposed bodies.

Serial sexual homicide has been going on in other countries, besides the United States. However, the US remains at the forefront of serial sexual homicide. Much debate surrounds the issues of the reason for this. One of the major reasons points to the entertainment industry, of which the United States is the leader by far.

One of the main differences between serial murder with a non-sexual base and serial sexual murder is that non-sexual serial murderers will sometimes use a firearm or some other type of weapon that would get the job done quickly. Serial sexual offenders tend to use their hands i.e. asphyxiation to enhance their fantasy by sexually aggressive means.

The use of a gun quite simply isn't sexually gratifying for lust murderers. They need to hold on to the experience a bit longer and watch the victim struggle before he or she dies. It's sadistic to watch the victim's last gasp of life finally end in your hands. It's this mere hypothetical conclusion that drives most serial killers.

Research on serial killers shows that three most common methods used in inflicting death were mutilation, strangulation and bludgeoning to death by an object Almost all the methods of inflicting death would qualify as being sex based. Please note: these statistical methods and results are not completely reliable for two major reasons: the first reason is the year this information was gathered; the second, most of the relevant information of the study was provided by serial killers themselves.

One of the main noticeable difference between regular homicide and serial homicide is not only motive but also serial sexual homicide victims are often mutilated, and this is rare in regular homicides victims. The psychoanalytic perspective behind the bizarre mutilations is intriguing. Theorists have stipulated that the killer has an unconscious wish to re-enter the mother's womb and explore the interior of the body, perhaps to regain his original innocence, lost to his psyche, or for secondary sexual wishes.

Most psychoanalysts will agree that a serial sexual killer's sadistic impulses stem from the aggressive or destructive elements of early child–mother relations. Essentially, theorists say that a pathological relationship exists between mother and son. The crippled relationship transforms into guilt. The guilt causes feelings of inadequacy and begins to form into an overall sense of evil. His own sense of evil is projected onto his female victims.

Some studies have shown that serial sexual killers have

average to superior intelligence. Organized serial sexual murderers tend to be of above-average intelligence, while disorganized perpetrators tend to possess lower than average intelligence.

Approximately twenty per cent of serial murderers have a history of psychiatric treatment. Also, it has been found that seventy per cent of men who committed serial sexual homicide had undergone some type of psychiatric confinement as a child. Yet the presence of overt pathology in serial killers is not very common.

Furthermore, research has found that psychiatric disturbance of family members was present in about half of the cases studied. Family problems related to alcohol abuse accounted for approximately seventy per cent, drug abuse thirty-three per cent, and family members with a criminal background was about fifty per cent.

Approximately sixty per cent of all serial murderers in captivity have some type of criminal history. Moreover, about forty-five per cent of serial murderers, in an additional series of studies, had committed previous sex-related offenses.

Research has also shown that perpetrators who commit sexual homicide have DSM-IV diagnoses such as Conduct Disorder symptoms that precipitate lying, stealing and assaultive behavior toward adult figures. Conduct disorder in childhood is the same DSM-IV diagnosis as Antisocial Personality Disorder in adults. Research also leads us to believe that that almost all killers have at least some symptoms of this disorder. The most common feature is a blunt disregard and violation of the rights of others.

Most serial sexual killers are heterosexual. However, some have been known to have a history of homosexual activity. The presence of sexual disorders and paraphilia tends to be high among these types of offenders. Interestingly enough, about half of the offenders, who do commit sexual crimes, have been found to have an aversion to sex. What these types of offenders enjoy is pornographic materials such as books, videos and magazines. Of course, these materials are less threatening to their egos. In other words, the killer does not have to perform sexually to appease his partner. As you can recall, this kind of offender is likely to have an extremely debilitating ego and he is not about to take a chance in crippling it further by having sexual intercourse, something he feels he is not real good at and can exhibit absolutely no control.

Serial sexual killers for the most part are well-mannered, reserved, timid, religious and somewhat prudish individuals. They really are not known to have bad tempers, however they've been known to profess an intense hatred towards women. It is this obsessional hatred mixed with sexual desire that assists in driving them to commit violent crimes against women. Keep in mind prostitutes are likely to be this type of offender's favorite target because of the relative ease of luring them in for the kill and appeasing their fantasy. Distinct serial killers without an obvious sexual basis may attempt to lure more challenging targets in time.

Chapter XXVIII
BIOLOGICAL MECHANISMS

With the advent of technology we'll hopefully manage to obtain more information on the biological causes of violent behavior as it relates to sexual serial homicide. Some of the current research points to the limbic structures of the brain, which regulates emotion and aggression along with the hippocampus, and the septum, which is known to be involved with memory and sexual functions as well.

Extensive research has concluded that serial killers have adequate prefrontal lobe functioning to regulate normal aggressive impulses whereas mass murderers lack these prefrontal functions. Quite simply, serial killers adapt and conform to a normal lifestyle on the surface because they are able to do so. This shows in their ability to hold down a job, to refrain from killing every person they see, and their ability to virtually blend in with society. Mass murderers lack this capability based on an intense emotional breakdown that has somehow, manipulated neurotransmitter functioning within the prefrontal cortex of their brain. This sudden neurotransmitter imbalance and momentary emotional breakdown allows them to kill everyone they see. They are temporarily unable to restrain themselves at that very moment.

Another point of view taken that may be responsible physiologically in mixing aggression with sexual arousal is that the limbic structure of the brain transmits messages of attack and that direct message intercedes simultaneously with messages of arousal. In essence, serial killers become conditioned to the messages released from the brain that signal sexual arousal simultaneously with aggression. Hence, in a physiological sense, the neuronal postsynaptic potentials that result from the release of transmitter substances such as testosterone excite the neurons and cause a chain reaction. Hence, it's the physiological manipulation of these substances that causes them to attack.

The process I've been referring to in the previous paragraph is an established electro-chemical event that is controlled internally by subcortical regions of the brain that takes place for approximately two to three seconds. Keep in mind that I'm referring to the exact moment the serial killer physically attacks his victim.

It's absolutely incredible what the brain is responsible for. We don't give our brains nearly enough credit when it comes to the physiological aspects of health, illness and death. It's said that our brains control whether we live or die. To understand how this works, take, for instance, the mythology of dreams. Some researchers agree that if we vividly picture our death in a dream our heart can stop beating as a result.

How does this happen? Our central and peripheral nervous systems are transmitting the messages of death to our brain. Hence, the brain can shut down the respiratory system.

Another example is willing your physical self to die either by unconsciously wishing it through depression, hypochondriasis or consciously willing physical death by alcohol consumption, smoking, stress, or by other slow means.

In the early 1920s one of the most intriguing experiments took place that would forever change the course of research. The experiment took place behind the walls of a maximum-security prison located in southern England. The subject was a middle-aged man who was sentenced to be hanged for treason. In the early 1920s hangings were often viewed by the public. The inmate was offered a deal by the British government. The deal was as follows: if the inmate agreed to participate in the unknown experiment conducted by a team of psychiatrists, he wouldn't be publicly hanged. However, he was told the terms of the experiment would certainly bring imminent death.

Rather than be publicly executed and embarrassed in front of his children he chose his course of death through the benefit of science.

The psychiatrists told the inmate they were going to blindfold him and tie his arms and legs to a metal pole. The subject was then blindfolded, with both his arms and legs tied to the pole. Finally, the experimenters told the subject what was going to happen. "Every last drop of blood will be drained from your body." Superficial lacerations were made on each side of the subject's wrists. The subject couldn't feel anything, including the needle that went into his wrists, because his palms were so tightly pressed against the metal vice.

His wrists were face down. The psychiatrists placed two buckets on the floor underneath the inmate's wrists. The subject could hear what he thought was his own blood draining into the buckets. Instead of hearing his own blood being drained in the buckets it was the sound of water droplets from the ceiling. Hence, the team of psychiatrists enhanced the water droplets even further by talking out aloud about the subject's blood draining from his body.

The psychiatrists went to check on the subject every hour. As each hour passed, the inmate's vital signs became weaker until he eventually couldn't speak. After approximately three and a half hours the subject was deceased.

Serial killers are able to show little or no remorse for their victims because they're effectively able to manipulate their limbic structures that regulate emotion. Just like in the experiment, if the serial killer closes his mind off to reality, then the reality of killing a person ceases to exist in his mental repertoire.

Chapter XXIX
INTRINSIC THOUGHTS

Serial killers' psychotic episodes of behavior are believed to be a gratification of their instincts, in which their existence is based on control, forcing them to deny others. Their capacity to exist depends on their distortion of reality and the masking of their identity. When the riddle they hold is solved and the ultimate fantasy is obtained, they will no longer be able to exist. The psychological disease, which causes the absence of morality, assumes an instinctive drive to kill again.

To partly understand the broad scope between the pathology of a serial killer compared to a normal human being would be the issue of our own general inability to grasp reality. Both normal people and serial killers cannot grasp reality directly. Essentially, humans model their behavior after others. This forms our ideas and later shapes our psyche, thus creating a metaphoric uniformity that explains our own existence within the depths of our own minds. It is our indirect use of models that creates or distorts our reality in our minds.

We must remember that reality is not an observable construct for which we hold its truth, in the hypothesis that it does or does not exist. Therefore reality is submerged into a subjective, contextual basis, unique to every human being. Somewhere down the line, serial killers are faced with either faulty human models, such as abusive parents, or faulty interpretations of phenomenological models, created from their own unique sensations and perceptions of the life that surrounds them.

Freud was partially correct in assuming that neuroses are caused by the conflict between subjective morality and inherent biological drives. If our biological drives are not being met at a specific time then we must compensate for their absence. If we're primarily guided by the moralistic code bestowed on us by society our true being can never be formed. Hence, we'll rarely be satisfied with ourselves and the activities life has to offer.

Society generally follows an ethical code based on moral judgment and God's written law. Hence, when one deviates from this code we refer to him as being abnormal. Since sexual thoughts and behavior cover a broad spectrum, one must possess an open mind while regarding the aspect of normalcy and sexual deviance.

When one presents himself with sadistic sexual fantasies he cannot help but reflect back on his life. Believe it or not, most deviant sexual fantasies originate in the deepest corners of childhood dreams and subsequent reality.

Normal people who think and behave according to conscious thought tend to view stimuli in the environment as an abstract construct, whereas serial killers tend to view stimuli in the environment and their relationship to immediate self-gratification as concrete. For example, if we have the desire to lift up a beautiful woman's dress in the middle of the street we wouldn't do it. Why? Because it's not perceived as consistent with God's law and man's law.

In this case both our ego and superego modulate the current maladaptive thought pattern either to lift up the woman's dress or leave her alone. If morality wins the impulse to raise the woman's dress becomes repressed in our unconscious. Hence, the repressed id impulse of raising the woman's dress becomes manifested in our dreams, or is even subconsciously acted out in the days and weeks to follow. Whatever the case may be, masturbation is a compensatory mechanism that allows one to act out a behavior without making it a reality.

For a serial killer, masturbation must be precipitated by thoughts of a violent act. Hence, he will either lift the woman's dress or commit an act similar to it. Acting out the fantasy to the greatest potential places emphasis on the perpetrator's concrete mode of thinking as it relates to the woman and his perception of what's underneath her dress.

We've been referring to some areas of sexuality as normal. However, we must be aware of what is abnormal. Most of my readers will agree it's against most cultural norms to sadistically brutalize and systematically rape women. But is it really? One important aspect to take into account is the timeframe in which one's beliefs originated. Hence, most behavior that one considers abnormal today was at one time considered normal. For the sake of this chapter normal intimacy includes but is not limited to the ability to have coital sex with a consenting partner.

One of the difficulties with most serial killers is that they're rarely satisfied with intimacy and "normal sex". One definition of "normal sex" is coital play where both parties feel stimulated. Serial killers need resistance in order to establish a comfort zone before and during a sexual act. Hence, it's very difficult for them to be sexually stimulated unless this need is met.

Serial killers don't care whether their partners are satisfied. This is one of the primary reasons why most of these men are unable to establish meaningful relationships with members of the opposite sex. The sadistic nature which is most evident in their antisocial behavior becomes ingrained in their ideological repertoire.

While inside the developmental pattern of violence a serial killer represses his true sexual impulses towards women. His constant overload of repressed material causes a conflict within. Hence, his aggressive impulses surface simultaneously with his sadistic sexual thought patterns. The perpetrator's experiential stressors trigger an immediate response consistent with his sexually sadistic fantasies. How does this happen?

The mind and body are on emergency overload from the perpetrator's pent-up anger and frustration. His fantasies are played out in the role of how he feels experientially. His subjective experience is significant at the time he kills his first and last victim. Most serial killers' fantasies are acted out more than anything else because they serve as temporary relief from anxiety, guilt, anger, fear and frustration.

We stretch our imagination to further understand the internal process of serial killers. The FBI has come the closest with its endeavor. Hence, most of the information comes from the lips of serial killers themselves already behind bars.

New prototypes increasingly make their presence known with different character-logical traits, experiential development and motives.

The FBI deserves credit for compressing motive to universal sexual characteristics based on fantasy. Even with the most advanced theoretical opinions it's impossible to predict whether one will become a serial killer or not.

As the human race manages its unpredictable bounds it gives rise to new types of serial murder with an array of different character-logical typologies of those who commit such crimes.

The dawn of this millennium has given rise to a new breed of violence. For example, the internet has already become a useful tool for pedophiles and perhaps serial killers. The naivety of young minds sharing the same technology with potentially violent men or women may be a difficult one for authorities to challenge.

Are we fools in the public eye when presented with statistics on violent crime? Is it really decreasing throughout the United States, or do the numbers reflect a decrease because everyone is in jail or prison? What happens when their prison term is up? What happens with their children who grow up in one-parent homes? We're building a lot of new prisons to house violent men. Yet what happens inside these institutions?

The answer usually is nothing. There's rarely any effective rehabilitation method and very little treatment offered for serial rapists, pedophiles and serial murderers. Violent young men are released from prison smarter than when they arrived. In most institutions they're allowed books and other outside privileges.

Violent crime is currently on the decline. However, like the stock market it won't continue. The serial killer ratio has pretty much remained stagnant throughout the years. However, I personally believe this will increase slightly over the years to come. Its center stage is directly in front of the media glorifying violence. Television and radio continue to grow more powerful and technologically advanced. Hence, many more people will respect their purpose and be lured in by the unconscious message they transmit.

The natural competitiveness of mankind will evoke new successes and failures within the human race. The traditional family will cease to exist in a culture built on everlasting change and prosperity. We are very likely to see small increases in serial murder. However, there will be large increases in crimes of passion, serial rape, road rage and assault crimes involving low impulse control.

We find ourselves right back to square one. What *is* it that drives a serial killer to kill time and again, with no remorse? Their rage is not re-enacted as a result of childhood trauma alone. There are other forces, such as physiological ones, which we have not yet understood. We are still in the dark ages, when it comes to predicting violence and understanding what makes the Dahmers, the Kempers and the Bundys tick. Perhaps in time, we will better understand the pathology of those who have gone mad.

I leave you with one last thought: violence is no more than a construct created in the mirror image of man. Subjective fear adds the breath of life. Fear is violence and yet violence evaporates fear. Hence, one can no longer fear when one is mentally dead.

REFERENCES

American Psychiatric Association, *Diagnostic and Statistical Manual of the American Psychiatric Association*, Washington, DC, American Psychiatric Association, 1952

Brittain, RP, "The Sadistic Murderer" in *Medical Science and the Law*, 1970, 10, pp.148–207

Brooks, P, Devine, M, Green, T, Hart, B, Moore, M, "Serial Murder – A Criminal Justice Response" in *Police Chief*, June 1988, 54(6), pp.37–45

Brown, JS, "The Psychopathology of Serial Sexual Homicide: A Review of the Possibilities" in *American Journal of Psychiatry*, 1991, 12(1), pp.13–21

Cartel, M, *Disguise of Sanity – Serial and Mass Murderers*, North Hollywood, CA, Pepperbox Publishing Company, 1985

Claridge, G, Clark, K, Davis, C, "Nightmares, Dreams, and Schizotypy" in *British Journal of Clinical Psychology*, Great Britain, The British Psychological Society, 1997, 36, pp.377–386

Crepault, C, Couture, N, "Men's Erotic Fantasies" in *Arch Sex Behav*, 1980, 9, 565, p.81

Cunningham, Mark D, PhD, Reidy, Thomas J, PhD, "Antisocial Personality Disorder and Psychopathy: Diagnostic Dilemmas in Classifying Patterns of Antisocial Behavior in Sentencing Evaluations" in *Behavioral Science and the Law*, 1998, 16, pp.333–351

Dietz, NP, "Sexual Sadism and Serial Crime", Conference of Sexual Sadism and Serial Murder sponsored by the American Academy of Psychiatry and Law, Tri-State Chapter and the New York Criminal and Supreme Court Forensic Psychiatry

Clinic, New York, January 20, 1990

Dietz, PE, "Mass, Serial and Sensational Homicide" in *Bulletin of the New York Academy of Medicine*, 1986, 62, pp.492–496

Dietz, PE, "Mass, Serial and Sensational Homicide" in *Bulletin of the New York Academy of Medicine*, 1986, 62(5), pp.477–491

Dietz, PE, "Patterns in Human Violence" in *Psychiatric Update: American Psychiatric Association Annual Review*, edited by Hales, RE, Frances, AJ, Washington, DC: American Psychiatric Press, 1987, 6, pp.465–490

Douglas, HE, Burgess, AE, "Criminal Profiling: A Viable Investigative Tool Against Violent Crime", Federal Bureau of Investigation, US Department of Justice, *FBI Law Enforcement Bulletin*, December 1986

Douglas, JE, Burgess, AW, Burgess, AG, Ressler, RK, *Crime Classification Manual*, New York, Macmillan, 1992

Douglas, JE, Olshanker, Mark, *Journey Into Darkness*, A Lisa Drew Book/Schribner, New York, 1997, Mindhunters Inc.

Douglas, JE, Olshanker, Mark, *Mind Hunter*, Simon and Schuster Inc, New York, 1995, Mindhunters Inc.

Drukteinis, A, "Serial Murder – The Heart of Darkness" in *Psychiatry Annual*, 1992, 22, pp.532–538

Drzazga, J, *Sex Crimes*, Springfield, IL, Charles C Thomas, 1960

Egger, SA, (ed.), *Serial Murder: An Elusive Phenomenon*, New York, Praeger, 1990

Egger, SA, "A Working Definition of Serial Murder and the Reduction of Linkage Blindness" in *Journal of Policy Scientific Administration*, 1984, 12, pp.348–56

Fox, James A, Levin, Jack, "Serial Murder: Popular Myths and Empirical Realities", 1999, in *Homicide: A Sourcebook of Social Research*, Smith, M Dwayne (ed.), Zahn, Margaret A (ed.), et al.; pp.165–175, Thousand Oaks, CA, Sage Publications, Inc., 1999xi, p.356

Freud, Sigmund, Rieff, Philip, Freud: Therapy and Technique, Collier Books, New York, Macmillan Publishing Co., 1963

Gerberth, VJ, *Practical Homicide Investigation: Tactics, Procedures, and Forensic Techniques*, (2nd edition), New York, Elsevier Science Publishing Company, Inc., 1990

Gerberth, VJ, Turco, RN, "Antisocial Personality Disorder, Sexual Sadism, Malignant Narcissism, and Serial Murder" in *Journal of Forensic Science*, 1997, 42(1), pp.49–60

Gosselin, C, Wilson, G, "Fetishism, Sadomasochism and Related Behaviours" in *The Psychology of Sexual Diversity*, Howells K (ed.), Oxford, England, Basil Blackwell, 1984, pp.89–110

Grinstein, Alexander, MD, *Freud's Rules of Dream Interpretation*, 1984, third printing 1986, pp.89–121

Groth, A Nicholas, Birnbaum, H Jean, *Men Who Rape*, New York, Plenum Publishing Corporation, 1979

Hazelwood, RR, "The Behavioral-oriented Interview of Rape Victims: The Key to Profiling", Federal Bureau of Investigation, US Department of Justice, *FBI Law Enforcement Bulletin*, September 1983, Vol. LII, No.9, pp.8–15

Hazelwood, RR, Burgess, AW (eds.), *Practical Aspects of Rape Investigation; A Multidisciplinary Approach*, New York, Elsevier Science Publishing Co. Inc., 1988

Hazelwood, RR, Harpold, AJ, "Rape: The Dangers of Providing Confrontational Advice", Federal Bureau of Investigation, US Department of Justice, *FBI Law Enforcement Bulletin*, June 1986

Hazelwood, RR, Warren, J, "The Sexually Sadistic Serial Killer", workshop presentation, Association for the Treatment of Sexual Offenders Annual Conference, San Francisco, CA, 1994

Headden, Susan, Kulman, Linda, "A Search for Clues to a Killer's Spree", US World Report, July 28, 1997, Vol. CXXIII, p.34

Hickey, E, *Serial Murderers and Their Victims*, Monterey, CA, Brooks-Cole/Wadsworth, 1991

Hickey, EW, *Serial Murderers and Their Victims*, Pacific Grove, CA, Brooks/Cole Publishing Company, 1991

Holmes, RM, "Profiles in Terror: The Serial Murderer" in *Federal Probation*, September 1985, 4(3), pp.29–34

Holmes, RM, De Burger, J, *Serial Murder*, Beverly Hill, CA, Sage Publications, Inc., 1988

Holmes, RM, Holmes, ST, "Serial Murder" in *Murder in America*, Thousand Oaks, CA, Sage, 1994, pp.92–128, 173–200

Jenkins, P, "Serial Murder in the United States 1900–1940: Historical Perspective" in *Journal of Criminology Justice*, 1989, 17, pp.377–391

Johnson, Bradley, R, MD, Becker, Judith, V, PhD, "Natural Born Killers? The Development of the Sexually Sadistic Killer" in *Journal of American Academy Psychiatry and Law*, Vol. XXV, No.3, 1997, pp.335–346

Jung, C, 1911, "On the Significance of Number Dreams" in *Collected Papers on Analytical Psychology*, Long, C (ed.), New York, Moffat, Yard, 1917, pp.191–199

Kafta, JS, 1980, "The Dream in Schizophrenia" in *The Dream in Clinical Practice*, Natterson, JM (ed.), New York, Jason Aronson, pp.99–100

Kant, O, 1942, "Technique of Dream Analysis" in *Dreams and Personality Dynamics*, DeMartino, MF (ed.), Springfield, IL, Charles C Thomas, 1959

Kardiner, A, 1932, "The Bio-analysis of The Epileptic Reaction", *Psychoanalytic Quarterly*, 1, pp.375–483

Kozenczak, J, Henrickson, K, "In Pursuit of a Serial Murderer" in *Law and Order*, August 1987, 35(8), pp.81–83

Kraemer, Barb, D, Salisbury, Sandra B, Spielman, Cindy R, "Pretreatment Variables Associated with Treatment Failure in a Residential Juvenile Sex-offender Program" in *Criminal Justice and Behavior*, June 1998, Vol. XXV, No.2, pp.190–202

Kramer, M, 1969, "Manifest Dream Content in Psychopathologic States" in *Dream Psychology and the New Biology of Dreaming*, Kramer, M (ed.), Springfield, IL, Charles C Thomas

Langevin R, "The Sex Killer" in *Rape and Sexual Assault, Part III: A Research Handbook*, Burgess, AW (ed.), New York, Garland, 1991, pp.257–273

Liebert, JA, "Contributions of Psychiatric Consultation in the Investigation of Serial Murder" in *International Journal Offender Therapeutic Comprehensive Criminology*, 1985, 29, pp.187–200

MacCulloch, MJ, Snowden, PR, Wood, PJW, et al., "Sadistic Fantasy, Sadistic Behavior and Offending", *British Journal of Psychiatry*, 1983, 143, p.2029

Mark, VH and Ervin, FR, *Violence and Brain*, New York, Harper and Row, 1970

Martell, DA, "Estimating the Prevalence of Organic Brain Dysfunction in Maximum-Security Forensic Patients" in *Journal of Forensic Science*, 1992a, 37, pp.878–893

Maskel, LA, "Stalking the Stalker: Potential Serial Murderers", presented at the 25th Annual Meeting of the American Academy of Psychiatry and Law, Maui, HI, 1994

McCrary, Gregg O, "The Violent Mind sponsored by Nova Southeastern University" in Proceedings of the Symposium on Serial Rape, Murder and Violence, Orlando, FL, February 1999, pp.27–28

Miller, L, "Traumatic Brain Injury and Aggression" in *The Psychobiology of Aggression: Engines, Measurement, Control*, Hillbrand, N and Pallone, NJ (eds.), New York, Haworth, 1994b, pp.91–103

Monahan, J, and Steadman, HJ, *Violence and Mental Disorder*, Chicago, University of Chicago Press, 1994

Mullen, P, Taylor, PJ, Wessley, S, "Psychosis, Violence and

Crime" in *Forensic Psychiatry*, Gunn, J and Taylor, PJ (eds.), Oxford, Butterworth-Heinemann, 1993, pp.329–372

Myers, Wade, C, et al., "Malignant Sex and Aggression: An Overview of Serial Sexual Homicide" in *Bulletin of American Academy Psychiatry and Law*, Vol. XXI, No.4, 1993

Myers, WC, Burgess, AW, Nelson, JA, "Criminal and Behavioral Aspects of Juvenile Sexual Homicide" in *Journal of Forensic Science*, 1998, 3(2), pp.340–347

Norbert, Nedopil, "Violence of Psychotic Patients" in *International Journal of Law and Psychiatry*, 1997, Vol. XX, No.2, pp. 243–247

Patterson, RM, "A Psychiatric Study of Juveniles Involved in Homicide," *American Journal of Orthopsychiatry*, 1942, 13, pp.125–130

Pinel, John PJ, *Biopsychology*, Third Edition, University of British Columbia, copyright 1997, 1993, 1990, Allyn and Bacon, Viacom Co., Needham Heights, MA

Podolsky, E, "The Lust Murder" in *Medico-Legal Journal*, England, W Heffer Publishing Ltd., Cambridge Medicolegal Society, 1965, 33, pp.174–178

Prentky, RA, Burgess, AW, Rokous, F, Lee, A, Hartman C, Ressler, R, et al., "The Presumptive Role of Fantasy in Serial Sexual Homicide" in *American Journal of Psychiatry*, 1989, 146, pp.887–891

Raine, A, et al., "Reduced Prefrontal and Increased Subcortical Brain Functioning Assessed Using Positron Emission Tomography in Predatory and Affective Murderers" in *Behavioral Sciences and the Law*, 1988, 16, pp.319–332

Ressler, RK, Burgess, AW, Douglas, JE, "Rape and Rape-murder: One Offender and Twelve Victims" *American Journal of Psychiatry*, 1983, 140, pp.36–40

Ressler, RK, Burgess, AW, Douglas, JE, Hartman, CR, D'Agostino, RB, "Sexual Killers and Their Victims: Identifying Patterns through Crime Scene Analysis" in *Journal of*

International Violence, September 1986, 1(3), pp.288–308

Ressler, RK, Burgess, AW, Douglas, JE, *Sexual Homicide: Patterns and Motives*, Lexington, MA, Lexington Books, 1988, p.139

Revitch, E, Schlesinger, LB, *Sex Murder and Sex Aggression*, Springfield, IL, Charles C Thomas, 1989

Roscoe, Paul, "Sex, Violence and Cultural Constructionalism" in *Journal of the Royal Anthropological Institute*, September 1995, Vol. I, No.3, pp.627–628

Schweizer, Peter, "Bad Imitation" in *National Review*, December 31, 1998, Vol. L, No.25, pp.23–24

Simon, RI, *Bad Men Do What Good Men Dream: Forensic Psychiatrist Illuminates the Darker Side of Human Behavior*, Washington, DC, American Psychiatric Press, 1996

Stoller, RJ, *Perversion: The Erotic Form of Hatred*, New York, Pantheon Books, 1975

The National Center for the Analysis of Violent Crime, Serial, Mass, and Spree Murderers in the United States: Search for Major Wire Services and Publications on Offenders Operating from 1960 to the Present, October 1992

The National Center for the Analysis of Violent Crime: 1992 Annual Report, Quantico, Virginia, FBI Academy

The National Center for the Analysis of Violent Crime: Criminal Investigative Analysis/Sexual Homicide, Federal Bureau of Investigation, US Department of Justice, 1990, pp.115–122

US Department of Justice, Crime in the United States 1994 – FBI Uniform Crime Reports, Washington, DC: US Government Printing Office, 1995

Wade, C Myers, MD, Blashfield, Roger, PhD, "Psychopathology and Personality in Juvenile Sexual Offenders" in *Journal of American Academy Psychiatry and Law*, Vol. XXV, No.4, 1997

Weinberg, T, Levi Kanel, GW, *S and M: Studies in*

Sadomasochism, New York, Prometheus, 1983

Weinshel, E, Calet, V, "On Certain Neurotic Equivalents of Necrophilia" in *International Journal of Psychoanalysis*, 1972, 53, pp.67–75

Yochelson, Samuel and Samenow, Stanton E, *The Criminal Personality*, Vol. I, *A Profile for Change*, New York, Jason Aronson Publishers, 1976

Made in United States
Orlando, FL
25 May 2022

18186650R10107